THE PRIMARY HEAD

Peter Mortimore is Professor of Education and Deputy Director, London University, Institute of Education. He was previously Professor of Educational Research at Lancaster University. He has been a teacher, researcher, member of Her Majesty's Inspectorate, director of ILEA research and statistics and an assistant education officer (ILEA). He is the co-author of *Fifteen Thousand Hours* (1979, Open Books) and of *School Matters* (1988, Open Books).

Jo Mortimore is an educational researcher and is the co-author of *Education and Disadvantage* (1982, Heinemann Educational) and of *Involving Parents in Nursery and Infant Schools* (1981, Grant McIntyre). She has worked as a teacher, lecturer and researcher, and as an Assistant Director (UK) for the Save the Children Fund.

THE PRIMARY HEAD

Roles, Responsibilities and Reflections

edited by

Peter Mortimore
and
Jo Mortimore

P·C·P
Paul Chapman
Publishing Ltd

First published 1991
Paul Chapman Publishing Ltd
144 Liverpool Road
London
N1 1LA

British Library Cataloguing in Publication Data
   The primary head: roles, responsibilities and reflections.
   I. Mortimore, Peter   II. Mortimore, Jo
   372.1200941

ISBN 1-85396-140-X

Typeset by Inforum Typesetting, Portsmouth
Printed by St Edmundsbury Press Ltd, Bury St Edmunds
Bound by W. H. Ware, Clevedon, Avon

A B C D E F G   7 6 5 4 3 2 1

Contents

Introduction

Although a great deal has been written about headship, there are few books that enable headteachers to speak for themselves. Yet over the last 25 years, in the course of our experience within the education service, we have been struck by the eloquence and, at times, passion, with which headteachers speak about their roles and responsibilities. We decided, therefore, to give a small group of headteachers from the primary and secondary[1] maintained sectors the opportunity to present their reflections on headship to the interested public: just how do heads view their roles and responsibilities?

Since we conceived that idea, the need for such an account has increased. The Education Reform Act 1988 (ERA), for instance, has reduced the power of local education authorities (LEAs) and, correspondingly, has increased that of individual schools. Within schools, however, these new powers have mainly been vested in the governing body rather than in the hands of the headteachers. In some schools this has created confusion over who does what and who carries the can when things go wrong! Governing bodies, after all, are made up of lay people who, while under the auspices of the local management of schools (LMS) initiative, hold considerable collective powers, do not bear the day-to-day responsibility for running the school. The General Secretary of the largest headteachers' union has suggested that 'governors, armed with their new powers, are seeking to manage rather than govern'.[2] This confused situation has exacerbated the already-difficult task facing headteachers. Just how difficult a task is apparent from the list of duties and responsibilities published as part of the Education Act 1987. The main responsibilities include

1. defining the aims and objectives of the school and setting these out in a school development plan;
2. management and organization of the school and the effective use of all resources;
3. development of a curriculum – within the context of the National Curriculum;
4. general discipline and welfare of pupils;
5. maintaining systems of record-keeping and communicating with parents;
6. establishing and maintaining good relationships within the school as well as with parents, governors and the LEA; and
7. monitoring and appraising the progress of the school and its staff and managing appropriate staff development.

To these already-onerous duties have been added the tasks of liaising with the governing body (of which the head is usually a member) over its new role in respect of the delegated budgets and its power to appoint and discipline staff and, most recently, of responding to the possibility of opting out of LEA control. All this contributes to the need for a wider understanding of the head's task.

We anticipated that the 1988 Act would figure prominently in whatever our headteacher contributors had to say. However, in order to provide a common format – which the heads were free to work around – we specified six major sections dealing with

- the background of the headteacher and of the school;
- the headteacher's personal philosophy of education;
- the organization and management of the school;
- the organization and management of learning;
- relationships; and
- personal reflections on headship.

We invited contributions from seven headteachers (five women and two men) whose schools we knew or whom had been recommended to us. They do not represent a random sample; they do represent, however, women and men of differing ages, cultures and backgrounds who are working in very different schools in various parts of England and Wales and, in one case, in the Canadian mid-West.

While, in the latter case, we ancitipated obvious differences, we were interested to see whether there would also be similarities with the British schools. In fact many common threads can be discerned from *all* these accounts. Despite individual differences of emphasis, no clear-cut distinctions emerged between any sub-groups whether distinguished by gender, race or age or by type of school, catchment area or local authority. In the final chapter in this collection we seek to tease out the common threads and to draw any lessons for other practising or aspiring heads or policy-makers at the level of local or central government.

We hope readers (whether from these groups or interested members of the general public) will enjoy reading the collection as much as we have enjoyed editing it. We feel privileged to be part of the process – a process that, in some cases, involved clarification by the heads of their attitudes towards careers, colleagues, pupils, governors and the education service in general.

At a time of such rapid change, these heads have been under considerable pressures, as may be obvious from their comments. They were all considered to be effective, yet most of them worried about coping with the changes. The assertion by Michael Fullan[3] (Dean of Education at Toronto University) that from now on change was likely to be continuous would not have reassured them!

Of course, in a collection of such personal contributions, where heads and schools are identified by name, there is bound to be a certain amount of inhibition that affects what is written. On the whole, we think these heads have been remarkably frank but we are conscious, as were they, that the repercussions of too much openness can be severe. In our view, the overall impression likely to be left in the minds of readers is positive. The contributors, in the main, are dedicated professionals inclined to take an optimistic rather than a pessimistic view of the future. That these people are so obviously concerned about the difficulties facing headteachers and schools – not least the unprecedented pace of change and the status and morale of the profession – is a serious warning to all of us involved in the system but, especially perhaps, to those with political responsibilities for the service. These are thoughtful and reflective headteachers talking: as editors, we hope that those responsible for the formulation of educational policy will be listening.

Peter Mortimore and
Jo Mortimore,
London, June 1991

Notes

1. See Mortimore, P. and Mortimore, J. (eds.) (1991) *Reflections on Secondary Headship*, Paul Chapman, London.
2. Hart, D. (1990) 'Viewpoint', *The Independent*, 25 October.
3. Fullan, M. (1991) *The New Meaning of Educational Change*, Teachers' College Press, New York.

Acknowledgements

In commissioning these chapters, we were conscious that our editorial demands were daunting: requesting seven primary headteachers – committed to the leadership of their schools at a time of great change – to pause for reflection. We wish to thank all of them for responding so splendidly to this challenge.

1
Chris McDonnell
Fulfen Primary School

Chris McDonnell was educated in south London and undertook his initial teacher training at St Mary's College, Twickenham, during the early sixties. On qualifying he taught for a year at an 11–18 comprehensive school in south London, moving to a secondary modern school in Leeds when he married in 1965. After five years he went to a newly formed 10–13 middle school on Merseyside as Senior Master and Head of Mathematics. During the early seventies he completed the Advanced Primary Diploma at Liverpool University. From 1975 until 1978 he was deputy head of a primary school in the Wirral.

He was appointed to his first headship (of a Roman Catholic primary school in Staffordshire) in 1978, where he remained for the next seven years. He then moved to an LEA-maintained 9–13 middle school where he stayed until the school was closed in 1988 under the re-organization plans of the LEA.

He is currently Headteacher of Fulfen Primary School, still in the Staffordshire authority. He has contributed to a number of publications in the field of primary mathematics and has recently published a book on the philosophy and practice of school assemblies. He is married with three grown-up children.

THE SCHOOL

Fulfen Primary School was established out of the re-organization proposals of the Staffordshire LEA for the Burntwood area, and first opened as a primary school in September 1988. The original pattern of educational provision had been three tier, with eight first schools, five middle schools and two high schools. As the school population continued to fall during the early and middle Eighties, it became clear that the area could no longer sustain a viable three-tier system. The option of maintaining a restricted form of the three-tier pattern was rejected, as this would have removed the option of choice at the high-school stage. A return to the primary/ secondary model was proposed and finally implemented for the start of the new school year in the autumn of 1988.

The consequence of the restructuring was the closure of a number of the first-school sites and a redistribution of pupils. In the case of Fulfen, this resulted in a primary school being established on the site of what was previously Fulfen Middle School. Although September 1988 saw the end of three-tier organization, it was in fact an 'interim year', for none of the primary schools were, at that stage, established in their final form. Those that had previously been first schools still did not have the full range of primary-aged children. The others, including Fulfen, still had pupils of secondary age, the remaining top end of the middle school. This gave rise to an establishment larger than that finally intended.

During our first year it was necessary to operate the school on a split site, using the premises of the Burntwood First School just down the road from Fulfen – a school that had been a feeder school to Fulfen Middle School during the three-tier period. Six class groups (the younger children already established there) were left in their familiar surroundings, with six staff, one of whom was my deputy.

At the Fulfen site, we had to accommodate the rest of the school. The top-two year groups (six classes in all) were organized to follow a middle-school programme. The six staff allocated to these pupils operated a structured timetable for the year to meet the demands of various specialisms. One consequence of this was that the six staff concerned became somewhat isolated from the development of good primary practice that was being undertaken elsewhere in the school. The start of the new year in September 1989 was, for them, another new beginning, with all the consequent upheaval and uncertainty. The younger pupils, who were class taught, were partly accommodated in the older first-school buildings, and partly at Fulfen. It proved to be an interesting year, with 20 teachers, from six different schools, teaching 470 pupils, on a split site, with our older groups operating a model of organization very different from the rest of the school. Apart from that, there were few problems . . .

Unfortunately, at the same time as we were experiencing the genesis of new organization in our own area, nationally the Educational Reform Act

(ERA) was beginning to be realized. The implications of the Act for the established primary school were (and are) considerable. For a school in our position, so recently formed, the Act only tended to serve as fuel for a fire that was already burning very nicely. The actual process of re-organization was a stressful experience for staff, who moved, in many cases, to a new age phase and who had to come to terms with the problems of primary classroom management that were wholly new. The arrival of National Curriculum Council documents by the van load added considerably to that stress, to the extent that, on one occasion, I was greeted in the staff-room with the comment, 'Could you please give us a break, Chris, just for a couple of weeks'. It was a remark that arose out of tiredness and frustration, not out of professional disregard for the detail of the Act. The personal-survival instinct is strong in all of us.

In our new school (because no traditions or routines existed) our initial concern was very much one of day-to-day survival. The solution of immediate practical problems was much more urgent than the major issues raised by ERA. An established primary school may well have been able to turn its attention to the detail of the Act; for us, there was no tradition of organization, the building was unfamiliar to staff and pupils alike, and the day-to-day detail implicitly understood by a school community had to be created rapidly. A glance through staff-meeting agendas from that period gives clear indication of the detail that had to be considered: for example, the establishment of a school fund, of a parents' association, parental help in school, accident procedures, pupil records, wet playtimes, lunch boxes, coat pegs . . . the list was endless.

Many of the staff had previously been middle-school teachers and had no direct experience of the younger children. They had to acquire the confidence to undertake organization of the primary classroom, meeting the needs of pupils across a much wider range of the curriculum than had been their previous experience. In one sense the very geography of the school helped us, for the open-plan teaching areas determined that staff had considerable contact, and those staff experienced in primary practice were able to pass on many of their skills in an informal and practical way. It was very noticeable that the staff shared their experience, irrespective of the allowance attached to their post. When I first met parents at an open meeting in May 1988 I mentioned that I was 'more concerned initially for the staff than for the children'. This surprised some of them. The establishment of good working relationships helped us meet the needs of the children in the classrooms.

By the end of that first year, with the older pupils leaving to go to secondary school, we were able to close the premises occupied by the younger children and so we moved everyone to the Fulfen site. This removed what had been a fault line across the school: the 'two-in-one' syndrome was over and we could begin to think about the establishment of a primary school on the one site, without the additional group of secondary-age pupils. The interim year was behind us.

We opened in September 1989, with a staff of fifteen and a pupil roll of some 350. We had taken over the premises of a middle school: a modern, brick-built, single-storey building of open-plan design, with slated pitched roofs and interior features of open, wooden, ceiling trusses. The site is surrounded by a good hard-surfaced play area and ample sports fields. To one side of the school is a large pond and greenhouse, this whole area having since been developed into a thriving, wild environmental area.

We serve a residential area (Burntwood) some 25 miles north of Birmingham, near to the cathedral city of Lichfield. This is a semi-rural environment, with open fields adjacent to the school grounds and within a couple of miles of the extensive Forestry Commission area of Cannock Chase. It is an economically mixed area, although the entire catchment is one of privately owned housing. The pupil intake shows a wide range of ability, as would be expected given the size of the school, although the problems associated with the concern for special educational needs are limited. There is only a handful of pupils who are not of white ethnic origin, mainly of parents who are the medical staff at a nearby hospital. For all of them, English is a first language and so we do not have to contend with the challenge of teaching English as a second language.

PERSONAL PHILOSOPHY OF EDUCATION

My own movement in education during the last 26 years has involved a gradual change from the secondary stage through the middle years to the primary sector. The majority of that experience has been within the voluntary-aided sector of Roman Catholic schools, with the last five years being spent as the head of two county schools. This movement, in both the professional sense and by way of personal experience, has offered a wide perspective on the nature of schools and their function within a community in four distinctly different parts of England.

The drift from the secondary-age phase towards younger pupils (for that it was initially) came about when I moved from secondary schools in London and Leeds during the Sixties to a middle school on Merseyside in 1970. During my time teaching in the middle school my concern for mathematics was tempered by an increasing interest in the way young children learn across the whole curriculum, and in the structures that support effective learning. My appointment as deputy head of a primary school was the natural outcome of that development. My first headship – of a Roman Catholic primary school in Staffordshire – lasted seven years and, although this was clearly within the pattern of professional progress, it was also to be my last appointment in a voluntary-aided school. I found this a period of some difficulty, as I tried to develop modern primary practice in a situation where change had not been a frequent visitor. Throughout this time I experienced nothing but support and encouragement from the officers of the LEA for the changes that were taking place. It seemed to me a pity that other forces were operating within the community that set up occasions of conflict when there should have been support and encouragement.

The issues raised by the very existence of the voluntary-aided sector are complex and often emotive. That voluntary-aided schools have fulfilled a great need and contributed much to the educational life of English education is without question: whether or not they will be able to continue to function in the coming years as they did is more open to debate. The pattern of our society is changing so rapidly that there is a danger that we can continue to meet today's problem with yesterday's solution and then stand back puzzled at our apparent failure. My work as a head in LEA-maintained schools, continuing my interest and concern for younger children, has offered very different and new challenges to me as a headteacher, and as a practising Christian working in a largely secular society.

Schools, I believe, are about people: the people who are there as volunteers – the staff; and the pupils, who do not have such a clear choice in the matter. It is the formation and nourishment of this 'community of interest' I regard as pivotal to the task of the head of a school. Many models have been devised offering explanations of the intended purpose of schools. The appointment of staff to posts with pastoral responsibility, particularly in the secondary phase, reflected concern for the education of the child as a person. It was recognized that the social circumstances of a family often determined the success or otherwise of the child in the school. We are now experiencing a strong movement towards the view of the school as an instrument for the delivery of a centrally defined curriculum, and many of the performance indicators that are being discussed reflect this emphasis. We might justifiably question where the pastoral concerns fit into this model. It is said that teachers are paid to teach, not to play at being social workers. I fail to see how you can ignore social issues, for to do so is to challenge the perception of education as a shared experience for the adult and the child. If that experience is to be honest and fruitful, then it has to be an occasion of sensitivity. To demand from a young person what (through personal circumstances) cannot be given, creates barriers to learning and limits opportunity for real growth. The balance of these issues has previously been a matter for local decision, by the headteacher and the staff of the school and, to a lesser extent, by the governors. The Education Reform Act has now very firmly altered the balance, with parents and governors having a much clearer voice in the development of school policy, and the National Curriculum Council, following legislation, directs in much greater detail than ever before the content of the school curriculum.

A school, and especially a primary school, is a focal point for a community that may have little else in common. Families who happen to live in the same area but who do not necessarily mix socially or through occupation, come together as their children start school. This is their new shared ground where, for a specific reason (the supported education of their children), they come day by day and begin to form new relationships. The head, therefore, has to foster and support such growth. That support is more and more also becoming a pastoral role, for school is one of the few places of contact where parents can still expect to be given time and space for personal discussion. The signals sent out by a school to its local community determine very quickly the perception that community has of the experience we call 'education'. We can reinforce a stated aim of supportive education, with parents and teachers exercising a partnership role, or we can drive a deep wedge between home and school and from our particular standpoints view each other with deep suspicion.

My perception of the task the head's role demands, therefore, goes beyond mere concern for academic progress. Because children bring to school each day the cultural fragment that, for them, is home, the joys and strains of family relationships, the comfort or hardship of their homes, I find it difficult to see how their circumstances can be ignored if the school is to be a co-operative agent with their parents in their education. We are not filling stations, in spite of recent legislation.

The concern a head has for the pastoral needs of pupils and their families should also be shared by the staff of the school, for it is they who, day to day, put into daily practice the agreed philosophy of the school. A head can dream of an educational Nirvana from within the confines of an office, and there the dream remains unless it is translated effectively into good classroom practice by the teaching staff.

The task of team-building can be defined in relation to the specific learning goals of the school. A number of teachers pooling their varied skills to achieve an identified objective have to agree on a common process whereby that end might be achieved. The headteacher has the responsibility of overall design that enables such discussion to take place. Given the frequency of interpersonal exchanges within the school day, the success or otherwise of such team-building requires careful attention to detail. The time spent chatting with staff (very often about matters far removed from education) is not wasted: it is part of the relationship web that enables professional exchange to take place in an effective and meaningful manner.

In summary, people come first. Unless both pupils and staff come to school in the morning with an understanding that each is valued first and foremost as a person, the quality of the experiences of that day will be diminished. The value of the person must be recognized by the society in which that person operates. The resulting alienation when such value is not recognized can give rise to frustration and resentment for the pupil, and disillusionment in the teacher. Both learner and teacher are engaged in an interactive partnership, the quality of which determines the success of the classroom experience.

SCHOOL ORGANIZATION

With a school still in its formative period of establishment, many issues remain to be decided. However, one particular matter that was addressed early on was the question of decision-making: how were major decisions to be reached? One particular path (that of independent policy determination by the headteacher) no longer has credence, nor should it. The understanding that decisions made as the result of discussion are more likely to be implemented effectively influences the route we have chosen to follow. It is not always possible, of course, to place every issue before the whole staff, but we have attempted to open to joint discussion major matters that will affect the whole school policy.

Every staff meeting has an agenda, with the opportunity for every member of staff to contribute to it. Pre-meeting discussion always involves myself and the deputy head going through the details of the agenda to ensure that we are both fully acquainted with any matter included for discussion, and that we go to the staff with common intent. A head and deputy have the right and responsibility to argue and debate an issue in order to achieve an agreed position. Initial disagreement does not preclude eventual agreement; it does ensure that thorough discussion takes place. The staff should have confidence that there is a clear and reasoned view being expressed. Each agenda item is numbered and accompanied by the initials of the particular member of staff leading that item. Minutes are taken of every full staff meeting, by a different member of staff each time, with copies distributed to all staff as soon as possible after the meeting. A time limit of one hour is set and is strictly adhered to. This pattern of formal, concise discussion has served us well, with a good record being kept of agreed procedures. It may well arise that a particular item requires greater time or the more detailed attention of a group of staff. For this purpose, smaller groups take on the responsibility for resolving an issue or coming back to the full staff with recommendations. This pattern (of a small task group coming together for particular discussion over a limited period) is one way to ensure participation and shared responsibility for innovation.

The incentive allowances available to the school allow us to operate with four 'B' allowances and one 'A'. The delegated responsibility for these allowances is for the management of particular curriculum areas: language, mathematics, science and environmental studies, with the 'A' post being set aside for the post of professional development co-ordinator (PDC), who reports directly to the headteacher. The continued in-service development of staff is a crucial aspect of management for a new school that was established at a time of fundamental educational change. With limited funding, priorities have to be set and a school policy agreed. This has been achieved through individual discussion between staff, the PDC and myself.

Our major problem, in common with most schools, is the creation within the school day of effective opportunities for discussion and planning. Some use of assembly time for this purpose is made during the week, but with the agreement that all the staff are present for the Friday morning assembly as an expression of the community nature of the school. Greater freedom of attendance occurs at other times in order to give some non-contact time for staff to use in a co-operative sense. In the same way, at the other end of the day, with two class-teaching groups in every year, the staff make their own arrangements at story time to release one of the two staff taking a year group. Given the detail we have had to attend to in the last twelve months, time management can only give rise to even greater problems as ERA is fully implemented. We are currently planning a one-day in-service programme for the staff to look at our effective use of staff time within the working day.

Crucial to the effective running of the school is the working relationship formed between the headteacher and the deputy head. Too often the role of the deputy in the primary school has been nominal, with consequences immediately evident within that school: poor, ineffective management and the stunted professional development of the individual. In the longer term, with the appointment of deputies to headship, they go ill-prepared for the responsibilities they have to undertake.

During the last couple of years, everything that has directly related to the day-to-day operation of the school has been discussed between myself and my deputy, giving both of us the opportunity to be professionally and personally honest (within the confines of an office) during the formative stages of policy proposals we wish to take to staff and governors. On many occasions such discussions have resolved issues that would have taken valuable time in staff meetings with the larger groups involved. In some ways this may seem to be an attempt to short-circuit staff discussion and so lead to staff meetings that were merely rubber stamps of previously determined policies. If, however, such discussion is seen within the general pattern of small groups offering particular input to the whole staff, then it is not a threat to the open policy of the school but supportive of it. An example of this process was a recent discussion on the possibility of vertical age-grouping as a solution to a problem of an imbalance of pupil numbers across two age-groups. Four staff, with experience of the age-groups concerned, examined the option. At the same time, I consulted with my deputy. Our pooled views were then presented to the full staff with a recommendation not to implement the proposal. Although it was discussed further at the full staff meeting, much valuable time had been saved by this initial examination of the issues involved.

The full impact of local management of schools is yet to be felt, for we will not have a fully delegated budget until April 1993. However, in preparation for that we are looking at our budget share, restricted though it is, as a joint staff responsibility. Expenditure is made in an open way that acknowledges particular needs and recognizes agreed priorities. The extent to which this is effective is, at present, limited; but at least the initial steps have been taken that move us in the right direction. My concern for the future must be the increased work load that the management of our own resources will bring. If the administration, on a day-to-day basis, gets in the way of the team-building and the personal contact I particularly value, then something will have been lost, and 'efficiency' might have been bought at a heavy price. The effective role of governors within this process has yet to be realized.

ORGANIZATION OF LEARNING

To understand how a complex society such as a school performs is, in itself, a complicated issue. Much has been written of various performance indicators that might be used to determine quality and progress. In many instances they demand a historical perspective in order that evaluation might be meaningful. The audit by a school staff of 'where they are' must have within it a clear element of 'where have we been, and what have been our immediate and long-term experiences prior to this date?' This is something we don't have, for (through the experience of re-organization) we are effectively developing a new school. It was with this in mind that I wrote an extensive report for staff and governors that summarized a number of issues and policies that had been examined since we started. If nothing else, it provided a benchmark for future reviews and it gave us an immediate statement of our 'history', brief though it is.

We deliberately avoided writing lengthy curriculum statements when we first opened, preferring instead to rely on the accumulated professional experience shared by the staff. Now, having come to terms with each other, having created a working school, we are in a much better position to begin to formulate written statements of intent for the implementation of pro-grammes of study that are realistic for our school and are able to take some note of the legal demands now placed upon us by the National Curriculum. I am sure that this 'organic growth' will result in a greater degree of ownership by the school community of its curriculum delivery in spite of the external pressures of the 1988 Act. In this way we may preserve the personal input that makes one school different from another and so provide a counterbalance to the external pressures for conformity.

The environment in which children are placed day by day influences their growth and development, for not only do pleasant surroundings make for a pleasant life but they also interact with and directly affect the nature and quality of the learning experience. Our teaching areas are open plan in design, allowing for co-operative teaching and an economic sharing of our resources. The identity of the year group is clearly emphasized by the shared geographical area within the school. This has advantages in that, for pupils, being in a particular class registration group does not preclude contact with other pupils of the same age. Likewise, teaching staff are able to operate in a co-operative and supportive way, sharing resources, experi-ence and specialist skills in an open and informal manner.

Given the wide background experience of the staff-room, no single ap-proach to classroom management has been adopted. Some staff are already operating an integrated-day approach to the design of the working day. Others prefer a more tightly structured approach to their classroom manage-ment, unwilling as yet to allow for a variety of activities to be undertaken concurrently. We may well find that the National Curriculum modifies many of our approaches to the learning experience of children in the primary classroom. It is preferable at this stage not to be prescriptive for, considering the extent of the change we have all been through, such an approach meets the current needs of the school – for forced patterns of teaching that do not carry the personal conviction of the teacher will be less than effective. One positive value of the open-plan design is that the various styles can be freely observed and exchanged in an informal and unobtrusive manner.

Parents often feel unsure at first of the open-plan design of the school. After walking round and seeing children and staff at work, many of their doubts are resolved. They have at least seen the school as it is rather than as a series of interrupted class groups as doors are opened and shut. A parent who was being shown round the school with her child once stopped me and said: 'We haven't disturbed anyone, have we? In fact, they don't realize we've passed through their classrooms!'

A policy of child-centred learning that starts from where each child is rather than a general overview of a year group will, it is hoped, be the thread that runs through the development of programmes of study in the next few years. Although it should be possible to meet the demands of the National Curriculum's content, the issues relating to assessment still give rise to considerable concern. Both the internal, continuous, school assessment and keeping of records, together with the external assessment at key stages 1 and 2 raise questions we haven't begun to answer. The concern must be that when the answers do come, they could change primary education radically in a way that many of us would not find helpful to children. If the process of administering such assessment gets in the way of our essential task (that of providing high-quality learning experiences for children), then we must seriously question the direction in which we are being led. The consequent conflict between professional judgement and political demand would not be in the best interest of the pupil population of our schools. The need for educational development that is co-operative and carefully paced should be the basis of our search for quality: the alternative is the reduction of our schools to the role of the production line, and at that point the word 'process' might as well replace that of 'education'.

This concern must be especially evident when we consider those children with special educational need. We have begun to identify children who require particular support and programmes of work are designed specifically to meet their needs. We can no longer do this in isolation from the demands of the National Curriculum.

RELATIONSHIPS

It should already have become clear that I place great store on the personal relationships within a school. During one of our very first gatherings as a staff, prior to opening the school in September 1988, one of the staff asked a very simple yet pertinent question: 'What shall we call the head?' The response it received – that I have a first name like everyone else – laid down an early marker that there was to be a degree of informality in our relationships. That has indeed been the case and has at no time got in the way of a professional relationship existing between us. Humour eases many potentially difficult situations and often allows people to be honest in the presentation of their views in a non-confrontational manner. Certainly the presence of a staff cartoonist has led to lighter moments that are shared and appreciated by all. I seem to have been as much at the butt end of such graphic effort as anyone else.

The staff-room is just that, a staff room, open to staff, both teaching and non-teaching. To emphasize this distinction, staff meetings are taken in the school library, where there is space for a full circle of comfortable chairs, and by difference of location a degree of 'formal informality' is achieved.

Although I had extensive experience of the classroom prior to appointment as a headteacher, the demands now made by the post in a large primary school preclude an extensive teaching programme. This should not, however, mean that I should lose contact with the art of the classroom, for it is in the classroom and about the school that I gain and keep street credibility. The support I can give staff by working alongside them can be worth more than many words spoken at staff meetings or extensive statements of intent. But the choice must remain with me; the input should be by design rather than by accident. Apart from the support staff might gain from an extra pair of hands, or the expertise that might be offered, the experience of pupil contact in the classroom also serves to keep my feet on the ground and prevents too many esoteric ideas taking staff to regions that go beyond the art of the possible.

Classroom contact time also gains the respect of the pupils and prevents me from being a 'big one' who lives in a room of his own, the presence who is the ultimate sanction, whose signature appears on letters to their parents and who meets them occasionally at assembly.

Parents

Just because children are present in a school building for a period of time each day they do not cease to be the responsibility of their parents, nor should their parents interests in their welfare and progress be ignored. One positive element of the 1988 Act has been to emphasize the need for a sound working relationship to be formed between parents and teachers, for parents are indeed the first educators of their children, the school having a supportive and more formally structured role to play.

On the understanding that the task is one of partnership, appreciation by the parents of the difficulties facing the school and recognition by the staff of family relationships can only serve to enhance a child's educational opportunity. Ignorance of circumstances can give rise to misunderstanding and consequent conflict. Discussion of pupil progress should be seen as a joint concern rather than one side checking on the other. Both school and home have a vested interest in the education of children.

The Fulfen Association has attempted to provide another dimension to this home–school partnership by being a focus for social events that go towards the gradual building of the community of interest. That such occasions have also raised money for the school should not be ignored. Unfortunately we may find that in the drive to support schools financially, such associations will lose the focus of concern for the community.

Within the school, parents have been encouraged to help, support and co-operate in many different ways. A register has been established of those parents who are willing to give their own time in this way. They have been able to assist in many ways, through the preparation of materials, printing, helping with small groups or accompanying pupils and staff on visits to museums, farms or outdoor education centres.

These arrangements have worked well and there has been a mutual understanding of roles. The fear of many teachers that such involvement might lead to difficulties in our relationship with parents has not been borne out in practice. When the system of support was first introduced, the ground rules were publicly stated and agreed to by parents, and a mutual form of consent was signed by each parent. Matters of confidentiality, the professional responsibility of the teaching staff and our overall concern for the safety of young children were discussed.

Certainly, those parents who have been involved now have a greater understanding of the classroom experience. Within the group of some fifty parents who offered help, some have made a greater contribution than others, which is not surprising. As the mutual confidence of such support grows, I would hope that a much wider base can be established for it.

Governors

As with the staff of the school, the governing body has had to go through a period of establishment and team-building. Supportive relationships between school governors, staff and parents will, in many ways, determine the success or otherwise of a school. Both governors and parents must feel welcome in the school and should know and be known by staff.

It is essential that governors are informed people, aware of the realities of the school, understanding the issues faced by the teaching staff and appreciative of the needs of the wider community. Such information will not come by osmosis. It is only through the establishment of an honest and open relationship between the headteacher and the governors that information can be exchanged and governors welcomed into the school community, for they are part of it, not an add-on. We have attempted to achieve this through invitations to lunch, to particular school occasions and an open invitation to visit during a school day whenever it is convenient. It is not always possible, of course, for governors to attend such gatherings during the school day. Such an invitation is not, therefore, a 'one-off' opportunity but is open, recognizing the circumstances faced by the business commitments of the governors.

Trust and understanding only come through the experience of working together. ERA is demanding a much greater commitment from school governors and this, in itself, is helping to form relationships as problems are examined by governors – often in sub-committees assigned to a particular task, for example, preparing a policy statement on lettings for consideration by the whole governing body.

Yet again, the head is the 'gofer' who represents the school to the governors, who helps to clarify issues, presents facts, reports on progress and who, in turn, receives support or otherwise for proposed developments. The quality of the information given to governors will, in large part, determine their response. Heads have only themselves to blame if governors, acting in ignorance, make ignorant decisions.

Our newly evolving relationship is an area that needs to be handled with sympathy and understanding by both heads and governors. As head, I am seeing my professional expertise challenged by the legal authority of governors now able to make decisions and influence the detail of school policy in a way not experienced before in the maintained sector. Governors, testing the new Act, may well look for opportunity to see just where the edges are. There is bound to be, therefore, some degree of tension, as various interested parties try to define their responsibilities under the Act. It is a situation that demands patience, courtesy and understanding, with the paramount concern of everyone being the quality of the educational experience offered to children.

Inspectors and advisers

The role of the inspectorate is also changing. We have had in recent years an advisory service which was curriculum-led by intention, and supportive of schools. I am concerned that such a valued working relationship may change and that the degree of change will not be a matter of personal choice by the inspectorate or desired by the schools.

As we test the air in the aftermath of our recent legislative hurricane, there is natural concern that a shift in emphasis may have occurred and that visits by the LEA inspectorate could now have unforeseen consequences, not always good. This, of course, needn't be so, if heads and the inspectorate work hard at securing a relationship that respects professional integrity and responsibility. At this crucial stage, when the outcome of so many hastily prepared and largely unresearched initiatives is unknown, a division between headteachers and the LEA's inspectorate is the last thing we need to add to our headaches.

That inspections of particular curriculum areas and of broader curriculum and management issues will take place is not in question. Handled with a degree of sensitivity by both school and inspectors, such inspections could indeed be supportive of the school and help to indicate new approaches our well-worn eyes in the staff-room or office have failed to notice.

The issues of accountability that are now being raised will only be resolved by our living through the experience. The danger at the present time, and this is particularly true in the case of governors, is that too much might be asked for too soon. If the head and the teaching staff are pressurized to meet the letter of the law in an unreasonable manner, there will then be no movement towards new common ground and little mutual understanding. Tension and suspicion will ensue. Creativity and a degree of risk-taking (essential sparks for good education) may be dampened to the point of extinction.

PERSONAL REFLECTIONS

'If I was going there I wouldn't start from here' might be the acceptable advice from a villager to an intrusive town dweller seeking directions for a country walk. But as a reply to a teacher seeking advice on professional advancement it doesn't get us very far. We all started our careers as classroom teachers, learning a craft, coming to terms with the manner in which young people learn and attempting to understand how and why they experience failure – so often our fault rather than theirs. It is this varied background and experience we bring to our own exercise of headship.

A school community is a place where a head can have considerable influence, in both a positive and, unfortunately, a negative sense. In the short term that effect is not always evident. It is sometimes said that the absence of a classroom teacher because of illness has an immediate crisis

effect on a school, which is rapidly absorbed as means are found to allevi-
ate the consequent difficulties. The absence of the headteacher, on the
other hand, may have little immediate effect, but as time goes by the
absence becomes more significant. If long-term decisions are left without
resolution, then staff can easily drift into a pattern of behaviour that is
individualistic and fails to take into account whole-school issues.

The head is, in fact, a reference point, a 'still point in the turning world'
of the school. It is the point to which staff, pupils, parents and governors
turn at regular intervals, seeking indication for new directions or offering
their own contribution to the continuing dialogue of school development.
Headship offers the chance to get something done.

The other side of the coin involves the tedium associated with any administrative job, the paper mountain that threatens to become a fire haz-
ard, with just one more form from an apologetic LEA officer or district
inspector seeking yet more facts for some obtruse file. The details often
take valuable time to find, require endless signatures and often seem of
dubious value to the educative process. Perhaps that was why one parent
greeted me recently with outstretched hand: 'Ah, the straight line and
scribble man' – referring to my signature seen on numerous letters home.

As we move into the nineties we seem to be caught between two worlds.
On the one hand we are practitioners who must service our own varied
needs in the course of a week, addressing a wide variety of tasks,
chameleon-like as we turn from one to another. The stress currently placed
on the headteacher is in part due to the lack of ancillary support that exists
in the primary school. On so many occasions if there is a job to be done, the
head has to do it. Yet, more and more, the management role is being thrust
on us, with little increase in the support services that such a role demands if
it is to be successful. If the head is to accept the extra tasks demanded by
ERA, the day-by-day support that is received is a matter that must be
addressed with some degree of urgency. Our own management of time
becomes crucial to our effective management of schools: it may lead to a
radical re-examination of our role within schools and a consequent distanc-
ing from some issues to which we have been traditionally close.

Too easily, and particularly in smaller primary schools, the headteacher
can become an over-paid supply teacher, covering the absence of sick staff.
Acceptance of this role presupposes that the head's work can easily be set
aside at will and taken up when opportunity arises. It makes a mockery of a
planned programme and removes the head from the general service of the
school. He or she has then to undertake a holding operation with one
group. Anything further happening that day receives scant attention, delay
often resulting in further long-term problems. Somehow we have to resolve

the conflict between the role of the head as the one who enables a school to work effectively and the head who has to function as a crisis manager, filling in the bits to make it work.

For me, as a headteacher, there is considerable satisfaction in designing circumstances that enable effective and enjoyable learning to take place. To set in motion a chain of events that eventually results in modification and change that enhances the quality of education is most rewarding. From day to day there is variety in the tasks that have to be met. But my overriding role as head must be that of enabler, seeking ever-new ways to make that particular school community more effective and responsive to the needs of the children it serves. When this works then it gives a great sense of achievement.

Above all, I believe, a head should have vision. We should have the opportunity to look beyond the immediate needs of the day, seeking a perspective on the future that enables our leadership to be effective. The broadness of that vision will influence directly the quality of the education offered to the children who walk into the classrooms. Lacking such vision, a school stumbles without direction, blown by the winds of change without control. Small wonder that the end result can be chaos, and a poverty of educational opportunity that sells children short. With clear, sensitive direction from the head, energies can be released in both staff and pupils that result in excellence. It is our responsibility to determine that direction.

Commentary

A crucial issue for McDonnell, in his second headship, is how to mould a new school community from the disparate groups involved in the reorganization. A challenge at the best of times, the situation has been exacerbated by what appears to his staff to be the seemingly inexorable demands of the implementation of ERA. McDonnell voices a concern that this Act and the accompanying regulations may result in an overly instrumental view of education at the expense of the pupils' social and pastoral needs. He also raises the issue of potential conflict between the professionalism of headteachers following established good practice and change that has been introduced, primarily, for political reasons.

Like many fellow contributors, McDonnell has to face the problem of how to carve out time for discussion and planning within the constraints of the already-crowded schedule of a busy staff team who are in danger of being overwhelmed by the volume of government paper from the two new agencies – the National Curriculum Council and the School Examinations and Assessment Council – as well as from HMI and the DES.

McDonnell does not under-estimate how important to the effective running of a school is a working relationship between the head and the deputy – an issue discussed by Waterhouse (Chapter 7) and highlighted by research on effective primary schools. The research found that deputies were crucial to the good running of a school but that some heads found it difficult to delegate leadership roles to them.

McDonnell comments that assessment of a school's performance needs a historical perspective, something that, by definition, a new school does not have. Clearly, in theory, the plans to make public the results of National Curriculum assessment offer a way to assess schools but, as can readily be seen, the different intakes to schools (in terms of family income, home conditions and the social class of parents) make such crude comparisons meaningless.

The value to the head, the staff and pupils of having a teaching head are acknowledged by McDonnell, though finding the time to fulfil this obligation becomes increasingly difficult. This is a dilemma also commented on by other contributors. In McDonnell's view, it is an issue related to the conflict between the head as 'crisis manager' and the head as 'enabler'. For the former one needs flexibility and calm nerves; for the latter, vision.

2
Dorothy Smith
Hyrstmount Junior School

Dorothy Smith was educated in Derby and undertook her initial teacher training at St Matthias' College in Bristol, between 1975 and 1978. On qualifying she taught for three years at a 7–11 junior school in Leicester, moving to a 3–11 primary school in Dudley, in the West Midlands. After 2½ years she was appointed as a deputy headteacher at a 3–11 primary school in Halesowen (Dudley LEA). During this time she completed the Diploma in Education in Multicultural Education at Newman College. Since January 1988 she has been headteacher at Hyrstmount Junior School, Kirklees LEA. Dorothy Smith is the first and only black headteacher in Kirklees. This is her first headship.

THE SCHOOL

Hyrstmount Junior School was opened as a new school in 1971. Its buildings are beautifully situated among extensive playing fields adjacent to the Batley Rugby League Football ground, close to the town centre of Batley.

During the past twenty years the neighbourhood has seen many changes as families from the New Commonwealth have settled in the area and are now well established. As a result the local shops now include an Islamic Bakery, Halal butchers, a variety of general stores selling fabrics and household goods and a newsagent selling Indian magazines. August 1989 saw the opening of the new mosque about ten-minutes walk from the school. The whole of the Muslim community in Batley took great pride in seeing the first purpose-built mosque in the area being established, where their spiritual needs are now served.

The school serves pupils from 7 to 11 years. Approximately 95 per cent of the pupils attending the school are from families that originate (mainly) from India or from Pakistan; all are Muslim. The building is semi-open plan and each teacher has his or her own classroom with a wet area that leads into a shared-activity area. There is a central hall and a school library. At present there are four mobile classrooms, which are to be replaced by a new purpose-built building, consisting of five new classrooms, new staff-room, home-economics area, audio-visual room and other attractive features. Building work is now in progress.

The pupils are taught in eleven mixed-ability, vertically grouped classes: five 9–11-year classes and six 7–9-year classes. In addition to the eleven class teachers, the staff consists of three full-time section-11 teachers who work in classrooms alongside class teachers, supporting the language development of our bilingual pupils; two part-time teachers who support children with special needs; and two full-time classroom assistants.

PERSONAL PHILOSOPHY OF EDUCATION

My philosophy is based on the recognition and understanding that all pupils are individuals at differing stages of emotional, intellectual, physical, social and personal development. My aim, therefore, is that our school provides the opportunity for each pupil to achieve his or her full potential in all these facets of development. The ethos of the school – its characteristics as a social organization, what it is like as a place to be in – has a major effect on the development of its pupils and staff.

I believe that the ethos should be one that raises the self-esteem of pupils. Teachers should have high expectations of all pupils. This is particularly important when working with black pupils, as so often our work involves breaking down regrettable stereotypes of black people and their children.

PARENTAL INVOLVEMENT

I believe a good school is responsive to its community and is not isolationist. It was essential for me, as a newcomer to Batley, to get to know the parents of the pupils I was to work with. It was important not to make assumptions about parents, the amount of interest they have in their children's education, their educational backgrounds and their skills in bringing up children.

My previous experience as a deputy head of a community primary school had shown me that it was best to build up my own picture of the parents rather than to make assumptions based on folklore passed on from one colleague to another. The question was, 'how was this to be done?' At Hyrstmount, a 7–11 junior school, it isn't usual for parents to bring their children to school and, therefore, informal contacts, to which I had previously been accustomed (with mothers in particular), wasn't easy. I enlisted the help of a neighbour of the school who was multilingual, and who knew most of the families in the neighbourhood. I asked her if she would introduce me to some of the parents. Together we visited homes and invited parents into school for informal discussions with myself and class teachers about their hopes and aspirations for their children, themselves and the school. As relationships developed some parents became involved in the classroom during the school day, helping teachers and working with the pupils. Most of the teaching staff were readily won over to the advantages for them and the children of this level of parental involvement, which also led to positive feedback into the community about the school.

On the retirement of the previous headteacher, I became only the second headteacher of Hyrstmount Junior School. Over the years the school had developed traditions and routines with which all the existing staff, at the time of my arrival at the school, were familiar – as many of them had taught at the school either since it opened or for more than ten years.

The school recognized that good home–school links are important but previous attempts to involve parents had met with difficulties. The reasons for this undesirable situation are not difficult to identify. First, in areas where considerable numbers of ethnic-minority groups settle, it is usually the case that most of the parents have a first language other than English. Clearly this makes for difficulties in communication between schools and homes. Second, the shortage of teachers from ethnic-minority groups in our schools can mean that the school is frequently unable to take the initiative in developing relationships with parents because of the lack of a mother-tongue speaker on the staff. Third, parents from different cultural, linguistic and religious backgrounds often regard schools quite differently from indigenous parents. They may have different expectations of the education system, a different understanding of what schools can offer and may not be clear about the aims and organization of their child's school. All these issues had to be addressed and new strategies had to be tried to encourage participation and involvement. Such differences and the difficulties outlined had led to apathy (at its best) on both sides.

My experience in my previous school had also convinced me of the value of having members of staff with the same cultural, linguistic and religious backgrounds as the pupils. As it was a community primary school, the first such member of staff appointed there was the home–school liaison teacher. She was an interpreter to aid communication, someone with an intimate knowledge of the cultural background of the parents, and was a point of identity and reference who was invaluable in establishing good relationships.

At Hyrstmount we do not have a home–school liaison post. However, the issue of the appointment of ethnic-minority staff was seen as a priority by myself and the governors, and was discussed at length. Some argue that appointing such a person is tokenistic and, instead, place emphasis on the quality of staff appointed, regardless of ethnic origin. Recognizing that there are black teachers who are well qualified, competent and able to produce work of quality, two teachers from an Asian background (one Muslim, one Hindu) were appointed to the school in July 1990: the first a probationary classteacher, the second a classteacher with an incentive 'A' allowance for assessment. The teachers serve as a model for our pupils. We also have a classroom assistant who was my first appointment to the school. She is a Muslim, lives in the community and is invaluable in assisting the school establish home–school relationships.

PAIRED READING

Our aim at Hyrstmount is to have an open and welcoming school that provides a framework within which parents can communicate with staff and the head in a spirit of partnership for the good of the pupils. It was with this home–school partnership in mind that paired reading was encouraged within the lower junior classes. The paired-reading programme not only assists in improving pupils' reading but it also helps considerably in improving links between school and parents. On arriving at Hyrstmount, I could have gained the impression that, because the community was not 'flooding the gates of the school', it was not interested in the work of the school or how the pupils were doing. But it became clear to us that our parents are interested and, given guidance on how to support their children, they are ready, able and keen to help. For example, one of our families whose parents do not speak English was not put off doing the paired-reading programme once they realized that, at the introductory meeting, there would be an interpreter. Once they had attended the meeting and had the scheme explained, they were very keen and volunteered their 18-year-old daughter to help their 8-year-old son. Soon whole families were becoming involved in reading: 2- and 3-year-olds would sit studiously with books in imitation of their elder brothers and sisters, and helpers included aunts, uncles and friends.

At our school, paired reading involves myself and teachers visiting homes to observe paired reading in action and to offer encouragement and advice. Staff visit homes in the autumn term of each academic year. Each member of staff will make four to five home visits. At the initial meeting for parents to launch the paired-reading project, parents are asked if they would like a home visit. Since paired reading began, staff have visited over sixty different homes. To date, only one parent has declined our offer. Staff talk enthusiastically about the welcome they receive in homes, which often includes a drink and something to eat. There are a few pupils whose families do not join the project and so we try very hard to ensure that these pupils have reading partners, either pairing with older pupils, classroom assistants or their own classteacher, to prevent them falling behind their peers. Pupils have a great deal of autonomy: they choose what they want to read and can change the book if they are unhappy with it. Also, paired reading is not limited to English; the dual-language books are the most popular in our school library.

As a new head it was important to familiarize myself with the day-to-day routine, school rules and procedures; this I did quickly, but as time went on it was clear that my main concerns were going to be with issues relating to curriculum development and classroom practice.

ORGANIZATION OF LEARNING

At Hyrstmount we work very hard to create an environment where pupils feel warm, secure and are motivated to do their best. Teachers are encouraged to make their classroom a stimulating and challenging environment that both excites and motivates their pupils. A rich learning environment is provided through good-quality displays of pupils' work, which challenge the whole class as well as being an important way of valuing the individual pupil or group whose work it is.

I believe the general appearance of a school is extremely important. One of my first tasks at Hyrstmount was to organize (with the financial assistance of the LEA) the refurbishment of the entrance hall in the hope that visitors, on entering the school, would feel welcome, comfortable, at ease and confident that the school would aim to meet their needs. It is well decorated and carpeted and easy chairs are provided. Photographs of all the staff (teaching and non-teaching) are displayed prominently alongside displays of pupils' work. Also displayed in the entrance hall are the following statements in English and Urdu that indicate, to parents in particular, some of our aims:

At Hyrstmount Junior we aim to . . .

- value our pupils' own language and culture;
- provide equality of opportunity, promote harmony, understanding and justice;
- provide a curriculum that is broad, balanced and relevant, and includes maths, English, science, religious education, art, design technology, music, drama and physical education;
- provide opportunities for pupils to enjoy extra-curricular activities, such as netball, gymnastics, rugby, football, book club and residential visits;
- encourage parents to be involved in the education of their pupils.

I believe that pupils learn best from experiences in which they have been actively involved, and if the work required of them is well matched to their needs and abilities. Objectives must be set for each pupil, which are challenging yet realistic and attainable.

Teachers are encouraged to use the pupils' existing experiences and build on them by providing new challenges in and around school. Pupils are given the opportunity to observe closely a wide range of objects, to explore and investigate a variety of situations and to solve problems. Pupils are encouraged to ask questions as well as answer them and are encouraged to take responsibility for the development and direction of their own work.

Classrooms in our school are busy, active places where pupils are seen working together, talking about their work and learning from one another as well as the teacher. Working collaboratively helps all pupils in the class. The most confident pupils are able to gain more understanding of the concepts they may have learnt by verbalizing them. Other skills, such as leadership, co-operation and the ability to listen are also developed; the more reluctant pupil gains confidence through being involved in the activities. Collaboration of this sort has to be well organized and carefully planned by teachers. Much of our staff development plan has focused on the areas of classroom organization to ensure that this active and collaborative approach to learning takes place and that the best use is made of the space, furniture and resources available to us. Classrooms are organized to allow for individual, group and class work to take place, and much of our work is topic based with an integrated approach.

The staff are encouraged to be concerned for their own professional development by reading, attending courses and by spending time discussing school philosophy and policy and the best ways of implementing them.

My aim has been to create an atmosphere in school that encourages teachers to work co-operatively and collaboratively and to have the opportunity to develop his or her full potential. It is encouraging to see that many teachers have developed positive strategies for dealing with problems and difficulties and that they work together to find solutions and support and help one another. By working together, staff have recognized the value of sharing the ideas and enthusiasm of colleagues, with the result that they are able to generate excitement and enthusiasm in many of our pupils.

At Hyrstmount we practise whole-school planning. The school development plan covers curriculum, staff development, governors, parents and the community, buildings and resources. Priorities are identified within these and the implications of the school plan at classroom level are assessed.

Language

As a classroom teacher in my previous schools, great emphasis was always placed on language development and, with the support of the staff, priority was given to the language curriculum. In the absence of a language co-ordinator at Hyrstmount it was left to me, with the help of the deputy head, to initiate the review of the language work of the school. This began with a look at the school's book provision. We needed to provide a whole-school reading environment where books were seen (by the children) to be a real, living part of the school. We began by looking at existing stock. Many books had to be replaced. They were worn out and unattractive in appearance; illustrations, vocabulary and language were often inappropriate. We chose a wide selection of books that would interest the pupils and meet the needs of the curriculum. Reading levels were taken into account so that all abilities were catered for. Many new books were bought. Books that portrayed positive images of women, black, Asian and other minority groups were considered a priority. Our aim was to avoid the purchase of books that reinforced negative stereotypes of certain groups. A corridor was turned into an attractive library, furnished with soft carpet, big cushions and plants. We wanted the children to be 'hooked' on reading and, in order to help with our promotion of reading, classroom book-corners and the new school library had to be inviting, cheerful and comfortable.

The pupils are now able to choose their own reading material from an extensive range of fiction, non-fiction, picture books and story tapes, as well as dual-language material. Pupils have their own personal booklets

where they keep a record of the book they are reading, and of who wrote
and illustrated it. There is opportunity for them to comment on the
material they have read.

Creative arts

One of the many concerns I have is that, with the variety of curriculum
changes facing schools and other reforms (such as local management of
schools), schools have to be very careful that the curriculum they deliver
doesn't become heavily weighted towards academic areas that depend
upon cognitive and intellectual achievements as measurements of success
and failure. We need to ensure that we deliver a curriculum that also gives
status to the arts. I believe that a curriculum that gives this status is necessary for all pupils because it allows for other essential areas of development.
For pupils with learning difficulties in what are known as the basic skills, a
broad arts curriculum has a particular part to play in providing the opportunity for achievement and enhanced self-esteem. For this reason, art
education will always remain a priority in school.

Two years ago the school embarked on a creative-arts project, which
involved the school working with a textile artist. The fundamental aim of
the project was to promote creative art work in the school (staff and
children had little experience of work in textiles), to explore and develop
cross-curricular work and to promote the role of art as a vehicle for
learning.

The major concern was to involve pupils and teachers in arts activities
that required their active participation. We (that is, the artist, the LEA
schools-art co-ordinator and myself) hoped that links could be made across
the art-forms into other areas of the curriculum (such as language) and that
the teachers in the school, whether directly involved in the project or not,
would be able to use the project to initiate or extend work in their classrooms. The project ran for a period of eight weeks. The artist worked in
school for one day per week. The theme of the work was decided by both
artist and teacher together.

Before the work began in school, a series of meetings was held to discuss
the aim of the project to ensure that not only would the pupils and teachers
benefit from the experience but also so would the artist. It was essential
that the classteacher of the pupils was involved at all stages of the planning
and development of the project. A full staff meeting was then held where
the artist, prior to her work in school, met with the full teaching staff and
showed her work. She talked about how she intended to work with the

pupils, and the staff were encouraged to contribute ideas and suggestions before the artist and teacher involved in the project finalized their planning.

Once the project began pupils and staff worked with enthusiasm and great purpose. Throughout there was an emphasis on first-hand experiences of quality and on collaborative group activity. The examples of pupils' work that were displayed around school as each week passed bore testament to the high standards achieved. It was important to share this work with parents and the wider community, and so an exhibition of the work was launched and ran for eight weeks in the Batley Town Library and Art Gallery. Because of the success of the initial project, we now have an artist resident in our school each year. Each project has involved a different artist. We have worked with a potter and painter as well as with a textile artist. Our projects involving artists in school have made a great contribution to a broad and balanced curriculum for pupils of all abilities.

MANAGEMENT AND ORGANIZATION

School management is no longer an individual and autocratic matter but, to some extent, a group activity, with the personal qualities and skills of individual members complementing each other and with some responsibility delegated and shared. This still leaves the head as the overall leader supported by his or her senior team, which reduces the pressure as leadership tasks are shared and others in the school are trained for leadership.

At Hyrstmount, the senior management team consists of myself, the deputy headteacher and the co-ordinator of the lower school. Both these members are released from their class-teaching commitment each Monday morning by one of the part-time teachers. This enables the senior management team to meet on a regular basis to discuss the work of the school (i.e. organizational matters, curriculum, pupils and parents). It also gives these two members of staff the opportunity to talk to each other, visit classrooms, observe teachers and pupils at work and work alongside colleagues in the classroom when required.

As well as the senior management team, other members of staff are involved in the management of the school. The delegated responsibility for the incentive allowances available to the school is for the management of curriculum areas: maths (B); education for all (B) (i.e. multicultural education, equal opportunities, anti-racist education); information technology (B); reading/paired learning (A); art and design & technoloy (A); humanities (A). Other areas are managed by teachers on the main professional grade assisted by the head: they are physical education, religious education and health education. Science is managed by the lower-school co-ordinator, and language by the deputy headteacher.

On one day each week after school, the full staff meet to discuss curriculum issues. There is always an agenda for each meeting, so that members of staff are prepared and feel able to contribute to the discussion. The meetings are chaired by myself or the member of staff responsible for the area of the curriculum being discussed.

In addition, year groups meet with their team co-ordinator to discuss their own agendas (which sometimes are shared with me) at management meetings on a Monday morning. This gives staff the opportunity to discuss the work of the team, relationships, use of resources, management of time, pupils, daily routine, special events and educational visits, etc. Information staff consider I need to have will be passed on. Sometimes I am invited to attend to clarify points or to offer my view on issues of concern.

Most of my work over the past two years has been to establish the management structure of the school, to establish a team approach to our work and to create a positive climate for all. This has not been easy. It has meant a whole new way of thinking for some staff, many of whom have been accustomed to working as an individual behind closed doors. With some staff taking early retirement and new staff arriving (including three probationers in my first year), we have had to get to know each other and learn to work together as a school. As head, my task has been to encourage a feeling of belonging to the team, mutual support and co-operation. In the main this has been achieved by working closely with receptive colleagues, establishing a way of working in the classroom, setting up models of good practice, teaching alongside staff and enabling curriculum co-ordinators the opportunity to visit colleagues' classrooms. Most staff meetings are structured to enable staff to work in pairs and small groups, thus developing relationships, sharing ideas and opinions.

A conscious decision was made that a short-term strategy would be to work with positive members of staff who were enthusiastic about the work and development of the school and who shared some common philosophy, in the hope that, in the long term, enthusiasm generated by staff and pupils in those areas of the school would permeate throughout. Having a strong commitment to the school and its development and maintaining a high profile around the school (i.e. not being confined to the office) was an essential factor in facilitating team-building.

Our school development plan has helped us to prioritize areas of the curriculum for development in a school year. We are a large staff (18 in number) so we feel able to target two areas of the curriculum at a time for development. In order to achieve our targets for the year, we agreed to organize ourselves into curriculum teams. These two teams meet fortnightly; each member of staff decides which team they wish to work in. In practice staff are fairly evenly distributed between the two teams and every member of staff contributes to the development of that area of work.

Working in this way has helped us to plan for change. The demand for change in the light of the National Curriculum has highlighted the need for a carefully planned programme of school-focused curriculum change. We have had to review the curriculum already offered to see where adjustments are necessary to meet the programmes of study and attainment targets. Adjustments are already being made in the following areas:

- Use of facilities and resources.
- The development of stimulating contexts for teaching.
- Appropriate teaching processes.

LOCAL MANAGEMENT OF SCHOOLS

April 1990 saw the introduction of local management of schools (LMS) in Kirklees LEA. This meant that all primary, middle and secondary schools that have 200 or more pupils received fully delegated powers to manage the resources covered by their budget allocation. LMS has brought significant change to our school, in particular the extra workload, although extra resources have been made available to the school to assist in performing new tasks. Extra resources include additional clerical hours and in-service training for the head, deputy head, governors and administrative staff.

As we began to develop our own budget proposals to present to the authority, our main concern was, would we be able to adapt to formula-based funding and maintain continuity in staffing and the curriculum? As it happens, we were in the fortunate position of being able to appoint additional part-time staff to support pupils with special needs (albeit on a temporary basis) and are hoping that next year, with money saved this year, we will be in a position to appoint a full-time class teacher to enable us to reduce class size.

It is difficult to state at this stage what the full impact of LMS will be on our school but one of the advantages realized so far is the scope it offers for increased flexibility and subtlety in the application of resources to support curriculum objectives. It also helps to be in the fortunate position of being able to delegate much of the administrative duties related to LMS to a competent secretary with experience of accounts systems.

PERSONAL REFLECTIONS

The philosophy and work of a primary school reflects the leadership and personality of the headteacher whom, I believe, remains the biggest single influence upon the character of a school. I see the head's role as providing clear leadership concerning aims and objectives and clear guidance concerning teaching and learning in the various curriculum areas, appropriate to the needs of the pupils. The wise head will formulate these in close consultation with staff, the various elements forming the topics for school-based, in-service training. It is vital that aims and objectives are clearly understood by all the staff.

All heads have a vision and long-term plans for all aspects of the life and work of the school. Having the vision is easy; the ability to lead staff through the necessary steps required to achieve that vision successfully is the challenge of headship. This is a challenge I enjoy. Headship has given me the opportunity to get things done.

I find the many administrative tasks that are forced upon the school, particularly those that have little to do with enhancing the work of the school, exceedingly tedious. Since I believe that the head's role is to be an educationalist rather than an administrator, I try to delegate as many administrative duties as possible.

The most enjoyable aspect of my work is being involved with the pupils, offering positive encouragement to their achievements. I always try to look for the good things pupils have to offer and try to help them overcome their limitations. At Hyrstmount we provide for the pupils an atmosphere that rejoices in success but in which it is acceptable to make mistakes and to learn from them. Each pupil is unique. They are my inspiration.

Commentary

As a black headteacher of a school serving an Asian and predominantly Muslim community, Smith draws attention to an issue of great importance for any head (but especially one in her position): the danger of too readily making assumptions about parental support, skills and education.

She is the only contributor to state the need to present pupils with a range of reading material free from race and gender stereotypes. Smith's dual concerns with parental involvement and language development come together in the school's paired-reading scheme. Like others before her, notably Tizard and colleagues[1] in Haringey, Smith found that parental determination and the willingness to involve other family members in the children's reading, overcame the difficulties caused by their own lack of fluency in English.

NOTE

·1. Tizard, J., Schofield, W. and Hewison, J. (1982) Collaboration between teachers and parents in assisting children's reading, *British Journal of Educational Psychology*, Vol. 52, Part 1, pp. 1–15.

3
Ron Morton
West Heath Junior School

Ron Morton received his education in an extensive range of educational institutions: from both single-sex and mixed primary schools, to a boys' boarding school, comprehensive school, co-educational grammar school, teacher training college, polytechnic and university. He entered teaching in 1969 and has since undertaken a post-graduate course at the University of London, where he acquired an MA in Education, studying education in urban areas and taking the specialized option of educational administration.

He began teaching in 1969 in an inner-city primary school, quickly acquiring a post of responsibility before eventually leaving to work in the English department of one of Birmingham's largest comprehensive schools. His next position was as Head of English (the school's official title for the post) in a primary school in the heart of Birmingham. In 1977 he was appointed deputy headteacher of a large inner-city multi-racial primary school. Following a short period as acting headteacher, Ron Morton left to become head of West Heath Junior School in January 1985.

Ron Morton is a core headteacher to the National Primary Centre. He has written for several educational journals and is the author of children's fiction published by Hamish Hamilton and Methuen.

THE SCHOOL

West Heath Junior school has 360 pupils aged between 7 and 11. It is situated on the southern outskirts of Birmingham between Kings Norton

32

and Longbridge. It has a main, single-storey building constructed in 1954, with additional huts and an annexe.

The school is surrounded by a combination of private and council housing, and has an interesting social composition. Most, although not all, of the parents are in employment: some have professional occupations but the majority are in manual and technical occupations. There is a large number of single-parent families. Only a very small percentage of pupils come from ethnic-minority backgrounds. Although there is a wide range of ability, most children display average capabilities but are reasonably well motivated.

PERSONAL PHILOSOPHY OF EDUCATION

I know for certain that I entered teaching with a distinct, albeit somewhat academic, philosophy of education, probably motivated by some altruistic notion that was tied to a sense of vocation. My early idealism regarding what I believed teaching and learning should be about was fed by the likes of Plato and Popper, Dewey, Bruner and Plowden rather than a particular leaning towards any distinctly ideological perspective. Eventually though, as experience of teaching gave me a context for my philosophy, I realized that my greatest indebtedness was not to the great thinkers and shapers of educational philosophy and pedagogy but to my family, the children I have taught, and their parents – and also to numerous colleagues whose ideas and practice often filled me with inspiration and occasionally with despair.

Perhaps more than to any other I owe a great debt to the first class I ever taught. This initial appointment was to an inner-city school where I was given responsibility for teaching a class of 11-year-olds of diverse ethnic backgrounds, some of whom were genuine immigrants. The children had already been categorized into the lowest-ability class of a three-form entry at a time when the eleven-plus examination meant that, in common with all other children who stood any chance at all, the more-able pupils were coached on a diet of English, mathematics and verbal reasoning, while, in the words of a senior colleague, the rest were 'to be amused'.

I resented more than anything the thought that I had entered a profession where I was merely expected to entertain, even though it is true that a good teacher has something of the performer as part of his or her psyche. But I remember thinking, surely my task is to move the boundaries of children's knowledge and experience and to play a part in the intellectual, physical and moral development of the whole person? However, I soon discovered that the advice was given with sincerity and was intended to assist my survival, for it seemed that not one of my new class was remotely interested in learning. If education had a value or purpose to it then it was for others and not for them, placed as they were out of the way at the top of the school building and in a former science laboratory (the school had recently been established in buildings that once housed a secondary school) complete with side benches, sinks and gas taps and with all the austere atmosphere a school lab built in the twenties could muster.

There was no doubt that I had my work cut out. Leaving school at the end of the day I actually looked forward to resting my head on the window next to my seat and letting the rhythm of the bus lull me into a soporific state. By Christmas I was asking myself what had happened to my high ideals and philosophy. I seemed to have found myself barely able to communicate let alone advance any child's learning. Older colleagues told me I was doing well, but I wanted to be more than doing well – whatever that meant. In my terms, far from succeeding I actually felt I might be failing.

For Christmas, Santa Claus brought me some new ideas and renewed energy. The spring term began with a new strategy. First, I needed to impress upon pupils that they had as much responsibility for their own learning as I had; that I would prepare lessons that sought to involve pupils, that would be of interest to them and above all have a sense of purpose. Whatever the aims of each lesson, those aims had to be communicable and communicated to all the pupils. Furthermore, I would expect nothing less than the highest standard they were capable of giving and the very least I would expect of them is that they also had high expectations of themselves and would give of their best. This was not a negotiable matter, this was how it would be. And the results would be shown to all who ventured up to the top floor to see us, for we would turn our shabby laboratory into a permanent exhibition of how capable we were. This was greeted with some scepticism by pupils who had, after all, been relegated to the second or, in their case, the third division. Attitudes changed when scrappy work was returned as not being acceptable and pupils with known opinions and sharp minds were pressed for answers in class discussions while ground rules were introduced for those who lacked a sense of orderliness and prevented quieter children from taking part. And so my earlier philosophy of education, born of intuition and held together through a rationale owed to others, was gradually shaped and re-shaped in the light of experience in attempting to meet the real needs and aspirations of myself as both a teacher and a learner and my pupils as learners and often as teachers.

Upon reflection, of course, what those early lessons were all about was the importance of, and the raising of, a child's self-esteem and his or her self-confidence and expecting children to take responsibility for their learning, to be assertive without being aggressive. None of these ideas were any more innovative then than they are today. Neither do I think that the philosophy that espouses such ideas belongs to any competing ideology or lies along a continuum between radical or reactionary notions of what education is or should be about. Other philosophies, when put into practice, might yield similar results. But that surely depends upon what lies at the heart of learning, namely the relationships between all concerned. There has to be mutual respect and trust between teacher and pupil. On the part of the primary-school teacher, there also has to be a sense of vision. For me, that vision focuses beyond the classroom and is about the kind of person who will have a contributing role to make in future society; who will be making or helping to make key decisions and will generally be responsible for my welfare when I reach my dotage. Therefore, to me as a teacher and headteacher, that means that personal, social and moral education has an important role to play in the education of any pupil and I particularly welcome the introduction by the National Curriculum Council of education for citizenship, and health education with its apparent emphasis on the personal and social model for dealing with health issues.

At this point I am reminded once again of my first class of pupils. What soon became apparent to me was that the home background, with its strong cultural ties, was of immense interest and importance to the pupils. It therefore seemed logical that, in the absence of any curriculum guidelines, this should form the basis for the class curriculum allowing me, as it did, to draw upon the experiences of pupils and to develop learning through a natural interest of the issues their experiences raised and through journeys into the arts, history and geography of different cultures. Teaching could, I hoped, thereby become a shared and relevant process.

Unwittingly, I had begun to develop what was in essence a form of multicultural education. I say 'a form' because multicultural education then had no real definition, whereas now it has various interpretations. For me, then as now, what was important was not whether children experienced making chapatis or rangoli patterns, played steel drums or learned Morris dancing – all of which have some place in understanding different traditions, values and beliefs – but, more importantly, children were equipped with the academic and intellectual skills that would allow them to compete in a society where racism and many other '-isms' existed. I never saw it as my role to argue the case for my pupils, but rather as my duty to enable my pupils to argue the case against racism for themselves and, wherever they encountered such prejudices, to be able to expose them for what they are. These skills meant that a rigorous academic approach with high expectations was essential. Parents of the children I taught have told me that they too have wanted nothing less.

As my career progressed, taking me to five schools (three in the inner city of Birmingham and two in the suburbs) and across the age-range from nursery to sixth form, the question I have always asked myself whenever confronted with a new situation is whether my philosophy and its expectations are transferable. The answer has always come later of course and, interestingly, the essential elements remain the same. However, what is particularly striking is that the same philosophy, based on a sense of purpose, involvement, sharing and expectations of commitment and high standards of achievement, has as much application to teachers in their role as classroom and curriculum managers as to children in their role as pupils. But just as pupils need to have a sense of value – of high self-esteem – for success to occur, so must teachers.

By the time I applied for a headship I genuinely felt that seven-and-a half years as a deputy head, the latter part spent as acting headteacher, had provided me with enough experience to make me believe that I could confidently lead a school. But not just that: I had an image of the kind of school where teaching and learning was interesting, purposeful and imaginative and I had a keen desire to make such a place a reality. What caught my eye, however, was not an inner-city school where the bulk of my experience had been, but a predominantly white school in the utmost southerly suburbs of Birmingham. 'Why?' you might well ask. I think my only reason is that which relates to my earlier-stated concern and curiosity: was my philosophy of education and the skills I have acquired as a manager and a teacher mainly in inner-city multiracial schools transferable?

Following a fairly rigorous process of selection I was appointed to the headship of West Heath Junior School. However, because of my position as acting headteacher at the time, I was unable to take up my new appointment until a successor had been found, and consequently I did not start at the school until January 1985 – a full six months after my appointment. But what is particularly significant about the timing is that one month after taking up my post the teachers' dispute with their employers began, which was to affect the school badly for the next two years. It was a truly devastating blow for any newly appointed headteacher.

ETHOS AND RELATIONSHIPS

Upon beginning my headship, like most newly appointed headteachers, I decided that I would take stock of the school, see what its strengths were and what weaknesses undermined its achievement. I was sensitive to the fact that, although I had a philosophy of education, the teachers also had their own and it was likely that some consensus existed that formed the basis of a whole-school philosophy. To begin with I intended to, and indeed did, ask only the simple question: 'could you please explain to me why you teach what you teach in the way that you teach it?' However, it must be said that the first two years of my headship can only be described as the worst two of my professional life. Often I wondered if the changes I sought would ever take place. Good days, when something seemingly wonderful took place, were perfectly counterbalanced by a day of problems, even regression. Sometimes what appeared to be a teacher's anxiety caused through fear of change undermined the progress and optimism of the previous day. At half-past three I was left alone in an empty school except for the company of the cleaning staff. I soon realized that there is rarely change without some degree of pain.

From the time I set foot in the school I was naturally curious about the existing school ethos and above all about the relationships in the school, and immediately set about looking for the clues that would tell me how the school ticked. More than anything, I believed that whatever I would achieve in the future would depend upon the relationships I formed with my colleagues, with the parents of the pupils and, of course, with the pupils themselves. Now the Education Acts of 1986 and 1988 make it imperative for headteachers to ensure they have the right kind of working relationship not only with their staff but also with parents and particularly with the governing body, whereas prior to that the relationship with the latter could be best described as having to be no better than that of a vicar hosting his own tea party.

I arrived at the school, like all newly appointed heads, without any kind of working relationship between myself and the staff. Good relationships, I believe, are those formed not through hierarchies but as a result of close personal communication and understanding. The teachers' dispute meant that at the end of the pupil day the school was empty. No staff other than ancillary remained on site. What is more, the teaching unions decreed that teachers would not co-operate with curriculum innovation where time outside of the teaching day was needed to assist its development. It was a strict work to rule. The entire teaching staff was unionized. As a head I became torn between my ambitions for the school and my loyalty to colleagues whom I believe (then and now) have a strong case for improved pay and conditions of service and an understandable sense of grievance and injustice. Nevertheless, these were grim and difficult times; some confrontations did occur, but they could just as easily have been as a result of many other factors relating to changing circumstances than merely the dispute. But the dispute meant that matters that needed facing up to could be

avoided because of the teachers' stance, and the dialogue essential to re-
viewing and assessing the needs of the school was made difficult because
relationships were slow to form as they had to be virtually on a one-to-one
basis. In retrospect, those relationships formed on such a basis during the
dispute have resulted in a deeper understanding of each other, so perhaps
it could be said that some good emerged from that gloomy period. I certainly believe that as headteacher I learned skills, both interpersonal, managerial and organizational, that ordinarily might have taken me ten years to
acquire.

ORGANIZATION OF TEACHING AND LEARNING

When I took over the school it functioned in the perhaps idealized manner
of a suburban English junior school of thirty years ago. The children sat in
rows, were attentive and quiet. Teachers were in full control and teaching
was a 'dignified' didactic process. Lessons were subject-based. Schemes of
work existed but there was no evidence to suggest that they were followed,
that continuity existed or that a curriculum framework acted as a guideline
other than in mathematics and reading. In the words of one teacher, there
was virtual 'curriculum autonomy'. Resources were poor to say the least,
and the school prided itself on still having texts and apparatus in use from
when the school opened in 1954! The school boundary in relation to the
outside world and parents appeared to be clearly defined. Parents informed
me they had limited access. The school had then, as it does now, a good
middle-ability band. Children proceeded to their next phase of education
able to read, write and were numerate. They had good manners, were
generally happy and were undoubtedly welcomed as a prized intake at
their secondary school.

Most of the staff were experienced teachers but, with the exception of
one or two, were generally lacking in experience of a variety of teaching
situations. Their average age was early-to-mid thirties and none showed
any indication of wanting to move on, except for the deputy head who
harboured a not-unnatural ambition to become the head of his own school
and was applying for headships. The school had a low profile and, until the
headship vacancy was advertised in the LEA bulletin, I was personally
unaware of the school's existence.

The question for me, as an incoming headteacher, was, is this school
achieving its potential? How and where can improvements be made? Naturally it is a question I still ask myself today, particularly in relation to school
reviews and school and National Curriculum development plans. From the

point of view of change it was a most difficult question. Why change something that was apparently 'working' and 'successful' was the common belief of the staff. On the other hand, parents I spoke to felt that the school could loosen up, especially creatively, and there was also a general feeling of somehow being excluded from the process of their child's education. Of course, much depends on what is meant by such terms. Nevertheless, I decided to conduct an initial audit of the school curriculum, of teaching styles and attitudes, the school environment, resources and – the management structure. (It must be kept in mind that this was conducted during the early days of the teachers' dispute when feelings were running high. No matter how subtle, discreet or amiable I was, I still felt a sense of 'him and us', which took a long time to break down.)

Within two months I had acquired enough information through what I had personally witnessed, through such communications as the weekly return of the abominable class-record book supposedly stating 'what teachers did . . . that week', and through what teachers had said to me, to suggest that the school – although running along nicely, thank you – was probably under-achieving given the capabilities of its pupils and the potential of its staff's expertise. Continuity was based on what traditionally took place in the classroom: virtually anything that took the classteacher's interest. There were five posts of responsibility, consisting of one for English, art, craft and design, science and a post for environmental science. There was no mathematics post, the position being temporarily taken care of (for the last three years) by the deputy headteacher. A lesser-paid post existed for special educational needs and one also for games and PE. In my opinion, the opportunities available to post-holders for making a contribution to the decision-making processes, even within the sphere of their own subject areas, were very limited. Expenditure was also very low. One-off allocations of small amounts seemed to be the only input into curriculum resources. This was very likely the fault of an under-resourced education service, yet it must be said that a seventh of the total capitation for equipment, tools and materials was spent on television and video hire and the booklets accompanying the programmes. The fabric of the school building was generally poor and internal decoration – an eye-watering orange and yellow popular in the early seventies, and the ubiquitous battleship grey – lay testament to the last painting having taken place over a decade earlier.

Visits by the local inspectorate were quite critical of the school, although whether those criticisms, if substantiated, could not have been made much earlier was never made clear. Their visits were usually fleeting, and I was nearly always left in a state of depression. Looking back, I realize that for some strange reason I would defend the school and especially the teachers' efforts, even though I knew that there was some validity in the criticisms. It was like a father defending his child who had just been called ugly, knowing deep down that his child possessed a shining quality that, given time, would one day expose the superficiality of the critics.

Clearly, a strategy was needed to address the issues and indeed the problems. There were, undoubtedly, what one inspector referred to as 'growth points', namely, confident children, well mannered and reasonably intelligent. Furthermore, there was evidence that some teachers were beginning to ask themselves crucial questions concerning what they taught and how. Indeed, 'what was taught, how and why' became the focus of the strategy.

There was a need to meet regularly in order to establish a forum for the exchange of information and ideas. Once this was established it enabled vital dialogue to take place and began to give people a sense of involvement as everyone's opinions and feelings were sought. And out of the forum also came a basic mechanism for initiating reviews. Clearly stated job descriptions were first discussed with post-holders and then put into writing, in which my reliance as headteacher upon the senior staff was expressed and therefore their role would in future be seen as part of a management team. Some re-organization of the posts was needed and an investigation into the skills, interests and real capabilities of the staff, so that hidden talents could be given the opportunity for expression.

I also asked the LEA to support the application for a secondment of the science post-holder and the post-holder for special educational needs to bring their skills up to date. Whether the LEA was unaware that two applications had been made I do not know, but both applications were granted. This was a boost to the teachers concerned and proved to be of enormous benefit to the school. It only added to my belief that a secondment for professional advancement, following a specified period of service, should be an automatic entitlement of every teacher.

Taking into account my still relatively objective views of the school and those of the local inspectorate, some frank opinions were called for about the tense and rigid teaching situations, the relatively narrow curriculum, the over-protection of the pupils, the strict adherence to a timetable, the general lack of any evidence of planning, not to mention any overall curriculum framework and the need to set challenges for pupils to aspire to. These concerns may sound harsh in the light of what has been said about the achievements of the school, and it is possible that some may believe that it is a case of another so-called progressivist ruining a good school, but it is my belief that any school can 'achieve' – the test lies in the actual quality of the achievement in relation to capability.

There was a need for the work to be planned. To begin with I felt it necessary for teachers to understand what and how planning should take place if it is to be an effective tool for teaching and an effective means of analysing the what, how, why and when of the curriculum. Up to then there was no real evidence of planning, only a class record book existed that, as its title suggests, was merely a weekly account of what was supposed to have taken place. It turned out that teachers themselves were as disenchanted as I was with the value of this book and so it was replaced with a class-planning booklet, requiring that clear aims and objectives (communicable to pupils) should be stated and classroom activities planned with particular references to resources and organization. Key concepts also had to be outlined and the necessary key language that would be introduced to the pupils. All of this was contained on one page of A4, on the back of which was the requirement for the teacher to evaluate the class work, stating what had worked and what hadn't and why they believed this to have been the case. (Shortly after the introduction of this method of planning I heard a teacher mutter under her breath that it was like being on teaching practice since I had taken over! I wasn't too dismayed by the utterance and remember taking it as more of a compliment.)

More cross-curriculum work needed to take place, with more practical learning situations. Essentially, what was being sought was that the skills in, for example, language, be given opportunities to be developed and practised through a wide range of experiences. This was certainly no attempt to water down the curriculum. On the contrary, nothing less was intended than to add rigour to the curriculum. Good paintings are not painted in sixty minutes and neither are stories written in a single period. The process of learning was given immense importance, but the quality of learning surely requires that the outcomes are no less important than the process.

The kind of teaching and learning expected meant that children would benefit much more by being organized in a group formation within the class. No amount of hinting or suggestion brought any change. In the end I had to ask that the new arrangement take effect by the following Monday! I am glad to say that, despite the need to convince further one or two teachers of the expected advantages, the new arrangement was adhered to and almost immediately the benefit of the additional space it created for teaching and classroom organization was acknowledged.

Other targets were set, differences of opinions had to be ironed out and consensus reached. Some concerns would have to wait; what has been mentioned are those matters that were prioritized. I wanted to unify the staff so that there was mutual support, a common understanding and approach; I wanted to extend the pupils' knowledge, skills and experiences; I wanted to enable pupils and teachers to enjoy their teaching and learning. In essence, I wanted teachers and pupils to have a feeling of ownership: a sense of involvement, interest, sharing and purpose.

The major breakthrough came through whole-school projects that necessitated collaborative planning. Health education, in particular, was chosen as a means of bringing about change in the curriculum. Initially, the health messages, it must be said, were of secondary importance. Health education, I reasoned, could be found in every subject area of the school curriculum and so it would be ideal for cross-curricular work. Furthermore, it was a new endeavour and perhaps not associated with old ideas. It offered scope for bringing in visitors (in a nine-month period the school worked with 23 different agencies, many of them belonging to the welfare network), had home and community links and, I discovered, could be generously resourced by South Birmingham Area Health Authority. Perhaps above all, the personal and social aspects of health education would necessitate sensitive yet open discussion between children, teachers and parents. A bonus was that for the two-weeks duration set aside for the project, the formal class timetable could be thrown to the wind and replaced with a more appropriate one!

It was a challenge to which the staff responded with some determination, even if the motivation might have been to disprove some of the earlier criticisms. The result was a resounding success. Everyone enjoyed themselves, the areas of study yielded results that showed children had really thought about the issues, and restructuring the timetable didn't affect either orderliness in the classroom nor imbalance in the curriculum. For the first time I felt the emergence of a common sense of purpose.

Of course, there is nothing like success to enhance a person's self-esteem, and at last I believed that here was something to build on. Following the success of the project – evaluated by the teachers with the assistance of the LEA's curriculum co-ordinator for personal, social and health education – there was no looking back. I think, however, that the real turning point came a year later when the LEA asked us to develop a model for integrating personal, social and health education across the curriculum and within the framework of a spiral development. A year after that the school began to receive national recognition for its work in the area of health education and particularly its whole-school approach. Indeed, in 1989, ITV made three films of the work of the school: two were part of the primary in-service programme and one was for the *Good Health* series.

Those major projects were the means of solving the principal challenges. Out of what was for the school a new consideration regarding the organization and management of learning evolved a more effective approach directly relating to the management and organization of the school. Undoubtedly we are now a different school from what we once were, and this is felt even more acutely now that we have fully delegated responsibility for our own management. Relationships are better. There is a trust established that enables delegation to take place knowing with some confidence that a professional person will complete the task in an appropriate manner. This is essential to me, as headteacher, now that my workload had added dimensions and time-consuming commitments under local management.

Through those early experiences I have become a strong advocate of a more holistic approach to school management. I see all teachers, even young new entrants, as playing a part in the managing of the school, yet few management courses or teacher-training courses actually direct themselves to this. Certainly the post-holders have specific responsibilities (all the senior ones, including the deputy head, are still in the school) and are particularly instrumental in preparing and implementing the National Curriculum, but the main so-called management decisions take place during a weekly staff meeting that takes place after school. I am a great believer in the brainstorm technique, for I am sure that a collection of minds is much more productive and inventive than that of a single person. I think this is particularly true if the thinking has to take place at the end of a busy day in the classroom.

PARENTS

Through our earlier work in the area of health education we began to build up our relationship with parents. As their involvement increased and we came to know them better, we were able to ask them to identify areas they thought needed improvement. But identifying is one thing, actually doing something about it is what counts if there is to be any credibility. The school report to parents was devised by asking parents what exactly they wanted to know about their child. Interestingly, many parents considered their child's personal and social development as important to know about as their child's academic progress. Similarly, parents are asked about the role they would like the school to play in sex education, about how they think the school environment can be improved and even to participate in the assessment of their child's work.

THE NATIONAL CURRICULUM

With the introduction of the National Curriculum the earlier work of planning the curriculum paid off. By the time the first guideline documents appeared there existed a curriculum framework that ensured continuity and development of a pupil's learning. As the content of the core subjects and, more recently, some of the foundation subjects was made known, a review or audit of what was taught seemed necessary. The post-holders played a leading role in drawing up the comparisons between what we already taught and what we needed to teach in order to comply with the Secretary of State's request and take account of the LEA's own curriculum expectations.

Today the curriculum is planned and reviewed by classteachers working in year-group teams. On average, fortnightly year-group meetings are held. These are quite formal meetings. Agendas are set by the teachers themselves and minutes are taken that are then circulated to all other members of staff in order to keep them informed of what has taken place. In common with many other schools, we are paying increasing attention to the programmes of study as a valuable aid to making sense of the statements of attainment. For it must be said that teachers, even very experienced ones, have been understandably overwhelmed by the amount of what is expected to be taught and learnt. In our National Curriculum presentation to parents, it is noticeable not only how interested they are but also how surprised they are at how much their child is expected to attain and what teachers have to do if they are to achieve the set goals. To all of them I give the reassurance that, first, common sense must prevail; second, each teacher is not responsible for the teaching of the entire key stage but only a part of the programme; and, third, that I am interested in children learning and understanding concepts well. I would rather they have a deep knowledge of certain things and develop skills that will enable them to approach areas of knowledge that are new to them than have a superficial and inapplicable knowledge of many things.

Undoubtedly, during these times of immense change, what I have a keener sense of, perhaps more than ever before, is the importance of not just leading the staff and, on occasions, being the arbiter and the key decision-maker, but of the necessity to be working alongside them. This is not especially easy bearing in mind the virtual simultaneous introduction of local management and the new computing, financial and management skills that have to be acquired. Sadly, a diversion of their time from the classroom is not the only sacrifice heads will have imposed upon them. For many headteachers the time taken up is at the expense of their families and this cannot be right. Nevertheless, I believe that our professional task (perhaps as employees if there is no real commitment to the idea itself) is to fulfil the expectations of the National Curriculum – the outcomes of which have yet to be judged.

The school is already taking note of the National Curriculum guidance document 3, which suggests that 'In due course, it is likely that schools will "throw all the attainment targets in a heap on the floor and reassemble them in a way which provides for them the very basis of a whole curriculum" ' (part 1, p. 1). I believe this is very much the direction the school is taking as we address whole-school planning within the context of the National Curriculum. It is also interesting to note that planning, and even delivering the curriculum, does not cause nearly as much concern as the assessment of a pupil's achievement. Assessment is not new to any teacher but as it becomes a more formal matter of judgement, with its eventual public statement of performance, much analysis of how assessment takes place and, above all, what is being assessed, and why and how it can be built into the planning, has taken up a great deal of teachers' time. Some experimentation has taken place involving pupils assessing aspects of their own work and also parents stating how they view their child's performance. The school has started to keep individual pupil profiles containing a variety of evidence relating to pupil performance: the most interesting evidence, and the most vital being the significant pieces of pupils' work. I, personally, see little to be gained by the current vogue of headteachers appointing teachers to posts responsible for developing assessment. I think it is a panic measure out of which it is hoped the problem will be taken care of. Assessment of pupils is the responsibility of all teachers for which there has to be a common format and consensus. But at the end of the day nobody knows the pupil better than the classteacher and the most important statement regarding a pupil's true level of attainment has to take into account the professional judgement and opinion of the teacher.

As a staff, we all agree that it is necessary to state our teaching and learning objectives well in advance. Teachers know up to a year ahead what the major areas for development will be. For example, the deputy head has already had a short secondment with the Rover Group. This experience and the contacts made will be put to good use as the school begins to develop economic and industrial awareness within the curriculum. All teachers contribute to the school development plan, which is finalized and 'approved' by teachers before being submitted to the governing body for final sanctioning.

LOCAL MANAGEMENT OF SCHOOLS

The school was fortunate in being able to prepare for the National Curriculum at the same time as becoming a pilot school for local management.

These twin yet interrelated developments heightened our awareness of the implications there are and of the relationship of one to the other. The focus of our preparations has been on the school's formal programme of in-service training, most of which is determined by recent educational initiatives and by staff identifying what the needs are for their professional development. Obviously, post-holders and the deputy head often take the initiative for they, after all, are usually the key links with the LEA-provided in-service training. There is a school code of practice that states that those that attend in-service do so on behalf of all the staff including the head and deputy. Therefore, they have a duty to report back to the staff and at least take them through the key areas. Sometimes these form the basis of whole courses, and so teacher days, when the children are not in attendance, or after-school sessions, are designated to them. Not all courses, which if school-based usually include outside speakers or facilitators, are concerned with the National Curriculum. One recent set of in-service education and training (INSET) sessions examined the implications of the Elton Report in the context of our school; another involving health professionals was based on how to facilitate the menstruation needs of our older girls.

Undoubtedly, the most significant change to my role as a headteacher has been the introduction of local management of schools (LMS). Between 1988 and 1989 I was a member of a support group to the two Birmingham primary pilot schools and soon realized that the implications for schools of managing their own budgets was likely radically to change not only the role of the headteacher but also the whole approach to school management. I could not wait to enter the arena; not merely because I perceived it to be exciting but because it was to be the unavoidable future and, I reasoned with a nervous governing body, to be involved from the start would be likely to yield plenty of support from the LEA and a clearer understanding of what LMS actually is about. In April 1989 the school joined the second wave of five primary schools to pilot the LMS scheme. A year later the school operated with fully delegated responsibility.

The essence of LMS is that of being able to plan and prioritize appropriately the needs of the school within the constraints of the formula-funded budget. It is not something that can be tacked on to the end of what already exists – although for the pilots, including my own school, the impression I had was that our inclination was to carry on as usual. Although the introduction of the Education Reform Act 1988 had already alerted the governing body to the changes, it was LMS that actually galvanized the governors into operating as a management body. Meetings became more frequent, arguments and discussions became more serious and decisions and outcomes became more accountable. If I had harboured any ambitions for personal autonomy, I would have come down to earth very quickly. LMS, however, suits my style of management; for those less inclined towards a holistic involvement and a broadening managerial role there is likely to be disappointment.

So far, since managing its finances, the school has been very successful. Prudent housekeeping, the setting of sensible goals and a measure of good luck and good health has resulted in additional material advantages and an increase in part-time support staff for teachers and the introduction of a foreign language for year-6 pupils. Above all, there is an exhilarating feeling about making decisions that you know will benefit the school. The transfer of certain powers from the LEA to the school means that the headteacher can have plans that can be achieved and, sometimes, dreams that can become reality. Although there is hardly any extra money involved, there is at least the ability to ensure that what is there is neither wasted nor misdirected. The decision-making process, therefore, is best served by including those who actually use the resources – this applies not only to the staff but also to the pupils. Of course there are times when, due to the lack of unanimity, the headteacher or governing body will have to make a decision. Such executive action should make clear the reasons for doing so, indicating that it is based on professional grounds related to needs rather than personal issues.

As a headteacher I find my thoughts are directed towards the dilemma and conflict of ensuring the curriculum is needs-led rather than finance-led. Also, the apportionment of my time has become increasingly crucial. The school finances are operated through an IBM computer via a Schools Information Management System (SIMS) software package. Despite the school secretary working extra hours, being placed on a higher grading and fulfilling the role of a school administrator most competently, I still have to give more time than ever before to monitoring and driving the school's finances. Therefore the management of time to ensure a proper balance between my administrative tasks, my pastoral duties and curriculum responsibilities is essential. Hence the need for the management approach to involve as many people as possible, not only because involvement stands a greater likelihood of enhancing the quality of achievement but also because through increased delegation the headteacher will be able to retain close contact with the teaching and learning taking place in the school, and the well-being of the staff and children.

LMS is clearly more than an added dimension or a new diversion. It is the present and future reality for all State schools. The aim of LMS is to

enable teachers, governors, parents and pupils to hold the destiny of the
school in their own hands. This means that schools will be judged by what
they achieve, within the available human and material resources, and how
they achieve it. Being successful in this is to me what marketing the school
is all about, yet it is precisely the area of marketing that causes me a great
deal of concern. It is not so much that I am against the notion of marketing
if it means communicating the school's achievements and meeting the expectations of parents, pupils and teachers – on the contrary. But what
saddens me is the increasing number of schools that are appointing so-
called marketing directors and using a variety of slick sales presentations to
sell their 'product'. For, above all, I perceive a danger that a school, while
upholding a set of values and code of conduct for its pupils, might well use
an entirely different code of conduct by which it enters into competition
against neighbouring schools.

Up to now under the present reforms, thanks to a relatively recent rise
in the birth rate, primary schools have not had to undergo the almost
desperate scramble for pupils that some of the secondary schools (particularly the less popular) have had to endure. Indeed, as a headteacher I
have welcomed the benefits to the school derived from the eagerness of
local secondary schools to court and tempt our pupils. For once, as we
now plan various joint enterprises with our secondary colleagues, the
term 'cross-phase continuity' has actually meant more than merely providing fairly limited information on our pupils about to enter secondary
school. The future may hold something different and then I believe that
primary schools, who already pride themselves on having excellent relations with the parents of children who attend the school, will have to
examine closely whether they are actually fulfilling the expectations of
parents – where the key to successful 'marketing' lies! This may well have
a significant role to play in the debate regarding progressive versus traditional teaching methodology, in so far as schools will have to prove that
whatever is being advocated really does yield the best results. So, those
invitations by schools to parents to share, in partnership with teachers,
the responsibility for the learning of their child, will have to take note of
whether parents are perceiving themselves as being duped into a role that
is in fact subordinate, the confirmation of which perhaps lies elsewhere in
the school – such as being invited to work alongside the teacher in the
classroom but being not given access to the staff room at tea break because it is out of bounds to parents. In future, the signals primary schools
communicate to parents about what schools do, the way they do it and the
boundaries within which they operate will have to be considered
carefully.

PERSONAL REFLECTIONS

Looking ahead, I regard the future with a mixture of concern and excitement. I am anxious that schools are not allowed a period of reflection and consolidation to absorb the changes that have taken place. At the time of writing there have already been three Secretaries of State for Education during an eighteen-month period and this only heightens my concern that the government of the day faces up to the actual problems of the education service and teachers in particular – namely the recruitment of quality teachers, the raising of teachers' morale, the provision of good school resources and the overall delivery of an appropriate, high-quality education service. The achievement of those goals would be aided by unity and concensus within the teaching profession and its various professional bodies and associations. On the other hand, I am excited by the prospect of having more authority to bring about changes the staff and the governing body think are important to the progress of children in the school but which, previously, did not figure in the LEA's plans or budget. Naturally I am curious about the development and outcomes of the National Curriculum.

I notice, too, that gradually a measure of common sense is creeping into the National Curriculum. The suggestion the National Curriculum Council has made about throwing statements of attainment onto the floor and constructing a school curriculum will, it is hoped, also be taken up by the Council in order to provide schools with a workable curriculum. Being a believer in the need to set goals within a commonly understood framework, it is my opinion that a National Curriculum of some sort was necessary. The one delivered into schools has the makings of a good one, but it suffers greatly in its present form from the lack of a coherent overview of a week in the life of a school.

My overall concern is for the government to take positive steps towards enhancing teachers' self-esteem and the morale of the profession in general. Improved pay is only part of the equation; conditions of service and particularly working conditions must improve. For this to take place it is essential for the government and the local authority to cease placing the responsibility at each other's door – and neither is LMS the answer although it might go some way towards the solution. In relation to this it is interesting to note how often schools are urged to take lessons in management from industry and commerce. Yet if one looks at the staff facilities and incentives provided by Sainsbury's, Marks and Spencer, Nissan or Volvo, there is a clear emphasis on the value of the worker to the company. There are various ways I have tried to address this at West Heath Junior

School, for example, by making the staff-room as pleasant an environment as possible. Eyebrows are sometimes raised by colleagues outside the school when they discover the staff-room has a microwave, cooker, toaster, a constant supply of tea, coffee and fruit juice and a dishwasher. But I simply do not want a professional staff to spend often-valuable time washing up and I think they have a right to sit in civilized surroundings rather than the cluttered shambles that so many staff-rooms tend to be.

Another example of caring for those who work in the school is that of a health-education policy that takes into account the health and welfare of the whole staff. I believe that it is quite wrong to place pressure on a teacher by expecting him or her to put the needs of the school above the needs of his or her family. If a teacher is unwell or is needed at home because of the illness of an elderly parent or child then he or she should not be in school. And I must add that this has never been abused. In fact, during the past four terms the school has called on supply cover for sickness on a total of only four days.

Meeting the needs of the staff can also mean meeting the needs of the school. The operating of a job-share scheme has great advantages and it surprises me that many heads appear to be wary of entering into such an arrangement. Our school has ventured into such a scheme in order for the school to retain the services of an excellent teacher who would have left teaching because a full-time commitment was too much for her as the mother of a young child. Not only does the teacher benefit but the school has also been able to secure the services of another excellent teacher, also the mother of young children, as the partner in the job share. (The school currently is attempting to open a working mother's nursery within the school, which will keep some casual places specifically for teachers called to supply work.)

Despite the many criticisms, some deserved and some quite undeserved, teachers and teaching receive from their many critics, I believe that what I and my staff do is worthwhile and important work. I feel privileged to be part of a caring community and to work with teachers who strive to provide a high standard of achievement so that pupils may continue through life with a confidence, devoid of arrogance and with a sense of responsibility for themselves and others.

I accept that, rightly, the school will be judged by what it achieves and how it achieves it. Within the forthcoming debate regarding the quality of education there is no doubt that the performance of headteachers will be at the forefront of that debate and that their skills will determine – perhaps more than ever before as control slips away from the LEA – the direction a school takes. Education is, and will be, an exciting arena during what is undoubtedly a new era where headteachers may well sacrifice some of their autonomy but gain in its place the power to bring about significant change. In our elevated and extended roles, what we mustn't lose sight of is the very purpose of our existence; and setting aside time to spend with our children and teachers could not only prove to be our salvation but also perhaps be the essential factor of our success.

Commentary

Morton raises interesting questions about which influences shape heads' philosophies and whether or not a philosophy is transferable across very different institutions. For Morton, as with McDonnell (Chapter 1), his own philosophy has been sustained by a vision of good practice.

Morton stresses the importance of teachers having high expectations of pupils, both in terms of demanding the highest standards of which they are capable and in terms of the expectations pupils have of themselves. Many research studies have focused on the presence of high expectations in schools judged to be particularly effective. HMI frequently drew attention to the presence of low expectations in schools they have judged to be far from effective.

Morton's experience of life as a new head, wishing to introduce changes into a school perceived by many staff as working well, is echoed by other contributors. There is no easy answer to this problem. Nor is it peculiar to schools. Any new leader joining an established institution and seeking to introduce change is bound to be faced with resistance. It is a considerable achievement if they can elicit support for the new ideas.

Although the demands of LMS prove taxing and time-consuming, Morton considers it an exciting and exhilarating undertaking. He believes that it changes significantly the role of headship. Morton is also positive about the introduction of the National Curriculum, believing it can provide a helpful framework within which teachers can plan their work.

However, Morton, like other contributors, is much concerned about low teacher morale, low levels of resourcing and the difficulty of delivering a high-quality service.

4
Miriam Wilcock
St Andrew's Church of England Primary School

Miriam Wilcock qualified from Whitelands Church of England Training College, London, in 1955. She taught for five years in Oxfordshire, Kent and Hampshire, prior to the birth of a son and daughter. She returned to teaching in 1961 in Grove (then Berkshire) and has since worked for Oxfordshire. Wilcock gained her first headship in 1981 at Stockham County Primary School, Wantage (200 pupils), and was appointed to St Andrew's Church of England Primary School, Chinnor, in April 1987. She has taught all age-groups within the 5–11 range and has enhanced expertise in the teaching of modern educational dance, physical education, creative arts and language approaches with children. In 1975 she gained a B Ed honours degree at Reading University. She is actively involved as a trainee and trainer with management development and training for the county.

THE SCHOOL

St Andrew's Church of England (Controlled) Primary School dates back to 1860, but a new site (single storey, flat roofed, with six classrooms) was opened in 1966. However, Chinnor was expanding close to the M40 motorway and a second building providing eight more teaching areas, built at the end of a 100-metre drive, was completed in 1970. Classrooms in the newer building each have their own cloakrooms and toilets; in the original building two pairs of rooms share cloakroom facilities. Both buildings have a centrally paved courtyard, one with a pond. These offer facilities for growing plants and shrubs or safe areas for keeping animals. All rooms

52

have some carpeted areas with tiled areas for art and craft work, the remaining space being of wood-block flooring. The separate buildings give us the advantage of two halls, both equipped with physical-education apparatus and with wood floors suitable for work in bare feet. School meals are cooked on the premises in the adequately equipped kitchen. The halls are used as dining areas.

The grounds are spacious, offering three hard-surfaced playgrounds, with some concrete play equipment, and paved and low-walled areas with seating. Playgrounds are surrounded by open grassed areas for football and other sports. Some 15 years ago parents raised funds and energy to build a one-metre deep, open-air swimming pool with changing rooms. Heating the water to the mid-70s has enabled us to swim from May to October in most years.

The school is situated at the foot of the Chiltern Hills and it is a ten-minute walk to the nature reserve on the hillside. Our 360 children, aged between 5 and 11 years, come from the village itself and from surrounding villages within a radius of four miles. This necessitates some children coming on county transport, which can create problems for activities beyond the end of the day. Children who attend the small school at the neighbouring village of Aston Rowant transfer to us at 9. Transfer at this age does not reflect the policy established in Oxford City, where children transfer from first to middle school at 8. I understand that our historical arrangements have more to do with the space available at Aston Rowant. Two years with us does present us with the challenge to ensure that these children are happily and effectively integrated into the school. St Andrew's is proud to have been one of the pioneering schools that have been welcoming physically handicapped children as ordinary members of the school. In addition we are the 'base' school for a unit for autistic children. These children, too, are integrated for varying periods of time into normal classes.

Chinnor is a village offering a variety of residences for those employed in London, High Wycombe, Aylesbury and the surrounding towns, in addition to traditional rural occupations. By 1974 the village had expanded to a population of over 5,500 and another primary school was opened. That school currently has approximately 200 children on roll. While it would be true to say that Chinnor is a village of young people, the long-established families provide a balance of tradition alongside them. Within the community are a large number of highly skilled adults who give freely of their time and energy for the benefit of the community, and children can find activities to occupy themselves throughout the week. However, the teenagers have a greater problem: the nearest town and sports centre is four miles away and there is limited public transport.

Families living in Chinnor tend to be in professional or semi-professional occupations. Once children settle in school many mothers look for opportunities to resume their careers. We have only a few families of multiethnic origin. Parental expectations for their children are high and interest and support in the work and activities of the school is always forthcoming. On the whole children are eager to learn, enthusiastic and co-operative. However we have our fair share of pupils with specific learning difficulties, alongside those who choose to opt out because of low self-esteem or who feel unduly pressurized by adult expectations and aspirations.

PERSONAL PHILOSOPHY OF EDUCATION

My philosophy of education stems from the training I received at Whitelands College where the emphasis was always on meeting the needs of the individual child. Children acquire skills and knowledge when the surroundings are stimulating and purposeful. When work and effort is celebrated and valued, the child's own self-esteem is heightened and self-motivation results. I have never been happy to over-emphasize competition, preferring to encourage each individual to become independent learners, setting goals for themselves. Invariably these goals are higher than those that might be set by the adults around them. Within a secure and caring environment children can learn from failures, they come to understand and accept positive criticism and grow from it. Again I have my training to thank for establishing this aspect of my personal growth and development. Positive criticism was built in to all my training practice and my acceptance of its value has encouraged me to listen to the opinions and suggestions of others, and modify my own practice as necessary.

I have always seen my responsibility as a teacher to enable the children in my care to develop as a whole. This embraces the social, emotional, spiritual and physical development, as well as the academic. I am concerned with children before they start school and after they leave the primary stage at 11. To this end I have sought vigorously over the last twenty-five years to create and sustain contacts across the phases of education and welcome recent initiatives that endorse this. Children have lives beyond the classroom and we cannot meet their needs if we show no interest or concerns for their activities with families and peers. The enrichment that can be brought into the classroom from the wealth of experiences children enjoy is like gold dust: it can add a dimension to learning beyond measure. It is with this firm belief that I have always encouraged the involvement of parents in schools and genuinely look towards them as co-educators, working with teachers, in the overall growth and development of their children.

I have always aimed to surround children with artefacts that stimulate questions and curiosity. I place great emphasis on the value of real experiences as aids to learning. While this has embraced visits from many professionals and artisans, I consider that taking the children out of the classroom on both day and longer residential visits to be invaluable. Children gain both meaningful academic knowledge and the social skills of learning to live alongside each other, friend or otherwise, in harmony and cooperation. An extended period away provides teachers and children with opportunities to get to know each other, developing mutual respect and understanding, in ways that are often difficult in the classroom. When I returned to teaching in 1966, I was privileged to work for a head who was a pioneer in residential field trips with primary children. I owe him a debt of gratitude for initiating me into the breadth and depth of children's growth and development that can evolve from these experiences.

Schools should be lively, busy places with the children engaged in purposeful activities. This presupposes the security of a firm underlying structure and organization that is understood and shared by staff and children alike. Planning plays an essential part in achieving this and is, again, best brought into practice when it is shared with colleagues and the children. Evaluation should follow naturally and become the foundations of the next stage in the planning process. This is my vision and, like all visions, does not always come as fully into focus as I might wish. The pressures and calls upon personal commitments, families, outside interests, friends, which we all experience, inevitably result in periods when we as a staff know that our ideals are not being achieved. No one likes to admit that ideals are falling short and some staff find it more difficult to face shortcomings than others. These are the times when true professional support and encouragement are brought into play, and when we attempt to challenge ourselves in the light of our objectives.

Children are born with a natural curiosity and from an early age ask questions continually. This is the instinctive way of educating ourselves and yet for many years it has been the teacher who has asked the questions. I am now convinced that the more we encourage children to pose the questions and see our role as that of unlocking the door to finding answers, the more readily are concepts and knowledge acquired.

Nothing can be built successfully unless the foundations are sound and secure. We have a responsibility to equip children with the basic skills of literacy, numeracy and oracy. The acquisition of physical skills is of equal importance. Children need to be taught how to control and command their own fine motor skills, to record experiences in writing and drawings that communicate effectively with others. The ability to express themselves in dance, drama and music should also become as natural as breathing. These are high ideals, to which I find I have to return to re-create for myself the principles on which I work from day to day. Sharing and sustaining these aims with parents and governors also proves demanding. Convincing some politicians and the public that we really are trying to educate to-morrow's citizens fully can seem an uphill task.

These convictions have developed as a result of thirty-five years of experience since leaving college. They have been influenced by all those with whom I have come into contact: teachers of many years' standing as well as students and probationers who have so much to give in terms of challenge to our established practice. Lecturers and advisers have enabled me to step back, rethink and then be encouraged to move forward. Parents and children seldom take things at face value and need to know the 'how, what, why, when and where' of all that we do in school. Interwoven with all these aims, I believe that learning should be fun. If I get to the end of a day and there has been no time for laughter I consider that I have failed.

ORGANIZATION AND MANAGEMENT OF THE SCHOOL

I clearly recall the words of a headteacher early in my career: 'My teachers teach most effectively when encouraged to develop their own skills and personal styles'. In the schools where I have worked I have seen the truth of this. Successful schools are those that have been able to appoint staff who offer a balance of skills and styles. In any group of people there has to be a willingness to give and take, to acknowledge and respect the contributions each can make towards achieving the aims of the school.

I consider the 'staff' of the school to be all those who work alongside the children: teachers, classroom assistants, secretary, caretaker, lunchtime supervisors, voluntary helpers and students. In any school this would be a large number of people; in our school, with the Autistic Unit that has a high adult-to-child ratio, it is even larger. I shall not forget my first staff meeting when I said that I would like to welcome all teaching and non-teaching staff. I stopped counting them through the door when I reached forty! We don't have routine staff meetings of this size – we'd never achieve anything – but it is gratifying to find that invitations to 'all' staff for specific occasions, from farewells to my keep-fit sessions, receive a similar response.

In the organization and management of the school it is understandably the full-time teaching staff who carry the greater responsibilities. In addition to the deputy head and the head of the Autistic Unit, four members of staff hold incentive 'B' posts and two hold 'A' incentive allowances. There are a further five full-time members of staff and we have a teacher who works for a day and half with some of our children who have special educational needs. Without the Autistic Unit, with its high ratio of both teaching and support staff, we have 104 hours ancillary assistance, of which 37 are secretarial hours. Under the flexibility of local management of schools (LMS) we have increased the total ancillary hours to 129, giving us 92 classroom-assistant hours a week.

In the last two years our numbers have dropped due to demographic influences, and we have 12 classes. To make the best use of the two buildings, we have re-organized into two teams, one for years 1–3 (as identified by the 1988 Act) and one for years 4–6. The Autistic Unit has its own building where specifically programmed work can be pursued. The co-ordinator of each team has responsibility for the delivery and continuity of the work of the members of the team. Finances are also delegated for the purchase of consumables and day-to-day equipment and resources. The use of halls, timetabling of ancillary staff, break duties and arranging for supply cover when staff are absent, all form part of the job specification of the team co-ordinator.

Responding to reports and publications from HMI prior to the 1988 Act, we had already seen the value of identifying the strengths and skills of individual members of staff in a consultative or co-ordinating role. Given our large staff it would be surprising if we were unable to name someone to co-ordinate each of the curriculum areas. In achieving this I am confident that we are well served in mathematics, science, English, information technology, music, humanities and religious education. But those who have undertaken to co-ordinate creative arts, physical education and special educational needs would admit to having a committed interest rather than a high level of expertise. However, we are supported with advisers and curriculum teams of seconded practitioners on whom we can call for advice and assistance.

In any school communication is of paramount importance, but in a large school with two separate buildings the need to implement strategies so that we all know what is happening, when, where and why, becomes vital. We hold a weekly staff meeting, from 3.40 to 5.00 p.m. In addition, while I take an assembly with their children, each team is able to meet together for half an hour every week. Team co-ordinators frequently find that they need to have further discussion and planning times during the lunch hour or after school. Curriculum meetings have proved to be a necessity, particularly as we have been familiarizing ourselves with the demands of the National Curriculum. At least twice a term I have a session with senior staff. Agendas are always set for these meetings at which the focus will range from planning school activities (such as sports days, concerts and productions) to discussions on specific aspects of our teaching, the curriculum, record-keeping, parental involvement and issues raised by governors, the LEA or government. Whenever possible, papers (we aim at one side of A4) are circulated prior to meetings. We circulate a daily bulletin to every adult in the school. This contains details from any member of staff, teaching or non-teaching, concerning activities that may be happening that day, requests, information, celebrations or commiserations. Despite all our efforts we still fall short and staff, secretary, cook, caretaker or children will be heard to say, 'But I didn't know anything about that!' Letters to parents are circulated as the need arises, which appears to be with increasing frequency.

Each teacher is responsible for the children in his or her charge and, as our teaching areas are separate classrooms, this tends to be as individuals. However, I have become increasingly convinced of the value of staff working alongside each other and every encouragement and opportunity is given for staff to work co-operatively. This may be classes actually working together in the hall, outside or within adjoining rooms, often involving the scheduled time of the classroom assistant, myself and/or parents. By teaching for at least one full day a week I release staff with specific responsibilities on a regular basis for half a day. This offers further opportunities for staff to spend time together in both a supportive and apprenticeship role. With the delegation of in-service monies we have been able to pay for some supply cover to release staff. Our classroom and welfare assistants play an important part in the activities in the classroom and their specific skills are also exploited.

I have yet to hear any teacher admit that they work in an establishment that offers adequate space – teaching, storage or otherwise. Compared to many, our rooms are spacious (while we can keep classes to around 30), offering flexibility, good display areas and some storage facilities. With the reduction in numbers we have been able to release two teaching areas. We have established one room for music, television and drama. Some of our multi-purpose staging is arranged there permanently. The other room has become our resource room. Over the past two years we have been able to establish good resources for religious education with a grant of £800 from a local trust. This has made us look critically at the resources for other curriculum areas and we have attempted to gather these together, catalogue and display them. It is not easy to decide what items it is sensible to store centrally rather than closer to hand, particularly resources that may be required in the other building. But this works well for religious education and we hope to invest more funds towards this end in the future. The rooms are also used for groups of children working with other adults outside the classroom, and for meetings of parents and others.

The school is heavily used on three evenings a week for evening classes organized by a community education worker. During the autumn term it is not unusual for there to be as many as 200 adults engaged in activities in classrooms and halls on each evening. This is clearly meeting the needs of the community but does present us with some difficulties when we want to be able to use the halls for school purposes in the evenings.

Almost ten years ago Oxfordshire established a scheme of whole-school self-evaluation. Every school in the county is programmed to complete this exercise within a given span of time. The first round, planned to take four years, stretched to five; we're now on the second round, which is also falling behind schedule. St Andrew's presented their first school evaluation to the County Council in 1983. When I joined the school in 1987 the document proved invaluable. I was able to discuss with the staff the changes implemented as a result of the process and consider those that still appeared to be outstanding. The greatest value of the exercise has been the long-term effect of teachers forming the habit of review and evaluation throughout the year. We have made considerable use of the devolved in-service funds (£150 for every full-time teacher), and of professional training days to release staff for additional training, to bring others with expertise to us and to utilize our own strengths for the benefit of each other. The school development plan enables us to identify those areas that need our most urgent attention and those that may be deferred for the future. Given time, we aim to address concerns.

Time – there is always a shortage of this commodity. It seems to matter not one jot how often we re-allocate time, the cry is always the same – we need more. The use of time is frequently on our agenda. With the regular use of the school by others in the evening, classrooms cannot always be left ready for the next day's activities so most staff are at school between 8.00 and 8.15. This is a time when the staff know they are able to talk to me. Several headteacher colleagues set aside one morning or afternoon when they will see visitors, in particular to show new parents round the school. This has become quite a time-consuming job, particularly as most people, quite rightly, wish to visit both the schools in the village. I know this makes sense and, although at the end of a busy week I am tempted to instigate a more formalized system, I also know that it can create resentment when people ring to be told the head is not available. So I do try to deal with issues as they arise. We plan the day in blocks of time, from 9.00 to 10.30;

10.50 to noon; and 1.20 to 3.25. Timetabling is kept to the minimum and covers the use of the hall (which is always negotiable and I can never be certain to see the same group of children in the hall on any one day) and other shared facilities. Not all staff find this approach as easy to accommodate as others and every effort is made to ensure that any alterations or demands are negotiated at least 24 hours in advance. On occasions when this does not prove possible tempers can become frayed and tensions rise. Teachers will plan the use of their time within the day to suit themselves and children will be encouraged to be involved with that planning.

LOCAL MANAGEMENT OF SCHOOLS

Under the arrangements for LMS we have had control of our budget since 1 April 1990. We have received sound training from the LEA but have still become thwarted with the haste and hassle of it all. We *all* seem to be learning as we go along and this is not the best recipe for confidence-building. The expectations now placed upon the secretary have grown enormously. We feel sure that we shall eventually look upon the computer as a help and a friend. However, as we struggle to familiarize ourselves with all the new jargon, software and extended responsibilities it appears like a sword of Damocles above us. Our budget was based largely on historic figures not all of which accurately reflect actual expenditure (so the finance team tells us). We also have 60 per cent of staff at the top of their salary and only 5 per cent below point 8 on the salary scale. It is, therefore, difficult to predict how many of the things we'd like to do, such as employing more classroom assistants, redecorating, improving resources, and so on, will be achievable. What is certain is that we shall have flexibility to make decisions to meet the needs of the school as we define them (and have to bear the consequences). In itself this becomes another call upon our time in terms of planning and negotiation with staff and governors. Until we have run for at least a year and can plan on actual figures we are erring on the side of caution.

ORGANIZATION AND MANAGEMENT OF LEARNING

Individual teachers have their own unique style in the classroom, and children benefit from this range of diversity in approach. All communities are made up of varied personalities and we all have to learn how to deal with each other's idiosyncrasies and foibles. Children also need to experience security so it is important that we have agreed policies on certain aspects of our activities in school. In terms of actual content of our teaching, our own curriculum guidelines and the more recent National Curriculum documents set the parameters. In our attempts to implement the programmes of study in the National Curriculum documents, staff are finding benefits and support from working more closely together and, in particular, with staff teaching a parallel class. Classes are currently arranged in year groups of mixed ability with two classes in each year. In most instances these two classes are adjacent to each other, which provides greater opportunities for shared activities and approaches by teachers. As with any group of people, this is explored more successfully by some pairs than others.

We also have agreed policies on discipline, respect and care of our environment and health and safety. Attitudes and parity towards other adults working alongside us, or within the school as a whole, are also emphasized. We feel it is essential that children learn to respect advice, assistance, support and discipline from all those who work with us. We take any opportunity to demonstrate that we seek and value the latter's contributions and hope that our attitude will be caught by the children. We are also anxious that specific threads within the curriculum, such as presentation and handwriting, are given due consideration. Finally drafted work, for display or mounting in handmade books, is double mounted and when appropriate may include some form of decorated border. All exercise books are seen as working documents, to be used for continuous reference and information. Our guidelines for handwriting consider the natural development of children's dexterity and provide a suggested approach to the teaching of handwriting. This includes an emphasis on correct letter formation at all stages, alongside the need to produce a legible, flowing script. We use the 'Basic Hand' style with an italic cut nib.

Within the classroom, organization will vary. When it is appropriate the whole class will be taught and may work together. For a greater proportion of the day, children will be working with a partner or in small groups. There will also be times when children are engaged quite independently on their tasks. Teachers are conscious of the need to vary the groups in which children work in relation to the task. Sometimes it is beneficial for the group to consist of children with different abilities. The National Curriculum places continual emphasis on the need to discuss, interpret and relate experiences to others to demonstrate understanding. Working with others can often present meaningful circumstances in which this can occur. At other times, of course, benefits are gained from children working alongside those of similar ability.

It has been our practice to follow an integrated 'thematic approach'. In addition to recognized curriculum areas we also aim to include practical and direct experiences, which include off-site visits whenever possible. It is encouraging to see that the National Curriculum documents lay stress on the need to take a cross-curricular approach. As we feel our way into these new demands, individual teachers are tending to follow the same theme as their colleagues with the same age-group. This enables them to offer support and positive, critical evaluation of each other's work.

Attainment targets, as proposed in the National Curriculum, present issues that form the basis for wider discussion within team or whole-staff meetings. We have yet to be introduced to the reality of standard attainment tasks and can only hope that they will accurately reflect the activities within the classroom and the skills, knowledge and concepts achieved by the children. In the meantime, we have begun to explore ways of tackling continuous assessment in the classroom and in this respect teachers are sharing their successes and failures.

I have always emphasized the need to build on what children already know and can achieve. In 1987 we began to look at the records we were keeping for each child. We realized that they were not sufficiently explicit. We began to devise new formats and spent time considering what it was we were wanting to record. The Education Reform Act 1988 (ERA) has given this impetus and we have been directly involved with the training being offered by the county on assessment, profiling and record-keeping. We have not finalized our system and I suspect that it will continue to be amended and modified for a considerable number of years.

While I am sure that it is right to integrate subjects, since this is the way in which we live, I am also wary of the dangers of searching for ways to incorporate areas of the curriculum in a contrived way. I attempt to avoid this pitfall by asking teachers to submit forecasts to me on a regular basis, at least half termly. I am then in a position to challenge any aspects of the planned work that might appear to be unconnected and to discuss modifications with the teacher.

SPECIAL NEEDS

If we consider children as individuals then, by implication, they each have their own 'special educational needs'. This terminology has become commonplace for reference to specific groups of children, those whose needs appear to come outside the framework of education presented to the majority. It clearly includes those who have physical handicaps that inhibit their education and also those who, given the same inputs as their peers, do not make progress. I am equally concerned that we do not overlook those who fall at the other end of the continuum, who have high academic potential. As a school we need to spend time addressing our strategies and achievement in this respect.

In addition to the teacher who works with us for one-and-a-half days a week, we also benefit from a member of the special needs advisory team who comes in for one whole day a week. These two teachers work alongside the classteacher, offering specialized teaching for children, identified by the teacher, on a one-to-one or group basis. Wherever possible this will be directly related to planned work for the class and will be given in the child's teaching area. The special needs advisory teacher has access to specialized equipment and resources, which can be used by the children. If progress continues to cause concern advice is sought from the educational psychologist who will also work closely with our support staff. One of our first lines of approach is always to seek the involvement of the parents. This has frequently resulted in home diaries. These take the form of an exercise book in which the adult working with the child in school records work done, books shared, specific teaching undertaken, particularly emphasized aspects, alongside suggested follow-up activity parents and child can do together. Comments are also made about the child's responses and attitudes. Teacher, parent and child contribute to the diary and, although the format outlined above sounds very formal, what actually emerges is an ongoing dialogue between those involved that serves to reinforce the shared responsibilities we have for the education of children. Diaries may become part of the planned strategy that, along with efforts to enable the child to set his or her own goals within their capability, can be genuinely celebrated with peers and become the motivation to move forward.

The autistic children are integrated into classes whenever it is possible. Some are able to join in for part of the day after only a short time in the unit class; others find the company of others too disturbing and may only be able to mix at social times, such as breaks and lunchtimes. When they do join a class they have their own assistant with them who, working alongside, enables them to keep on task. The level of improvement achieved by these children can be attributed to caring and devoted personnel (teachers, assistants, many in the medical profession and the parents and supporters of the group). The specialized teaching that has been pursued can truly be said to be pioneering. It embraces the Waldon Theory of How Children Learn, Music, Drama and Welch Holding Therapies to address difficulties related to behaviour, language and learning. Welch Holding is about strengthening the bonds of love between a mother and child, which are the foundation of happy and healthy development. Held safely in mother's arms the autistic child learns to overcome his or her fear of direct eye contact and close containment. The theory is offered for those parents who want to participate. Sessions are held once a week and are part of the 'parents as partners' support service. This unique integrated approach to the teaching and support of autistic children has received international acclaim and the staff have been invited to give seminars and lectures at conferences throughout England and in Europe. We receive visitors and students from many institutions, as close as Oxford and as far away as Japan. Because these children are in continuous contact with children in mainstream school they do have models to imitate, which helps them towards overcoming their own difficulties. Having them with us also enables our children to develop sensitive and supportive attitudes towards all whose behaviour, for whatever reason, might deviate from the norm.

Our two physically handicapped children (one almost blind, the other with cerebral palsy) are fully integrated in a mainstream class, with full-time welfare assistants. These women have no specialized training but are totally committed to their task. The assistant working with the blind child has taught herself Braille to enable her to meet his needs. Support and advice is given by speech, physio- and occupational therapists in addition to the special needs support team in the authority. There is very little which the children do not tackle, from participating in productions and sports, to producing work to share with others like every other child in the class. Until now it has been Oxfordshire's policy to hold a 'statement' for children with special educational needs only if they attend one of the special schools in the authority. A 'statement' identifies the special needs of a child as perceived by a range of professionals, educational, medical, social, the parents and any others involved with the child. These may then be quantified and equated with some financial input, which can be transferred to the school's devolved budget. Children with specific learning difficulties or physical handicaps who are taught and integrated in mainstream schools have been monitored within the special needs service and supported as appropriate. In practice, this has frequently led to a compromise between the provision as perceived by the school and resourcing available from the authority. This will change with the implementation of LMS because a larger proportion of the total finances for education has to be devolved to schools. We do not anticipate that this will necessarily resolve dilemmas relating to special needs provision as we have been informed quite categorically that a 'statement' does not automatically carry with it any additional funding.

Although this level of input for children needing additional support might appear to some to be generous, we still find that we have to concentrate on those with severest need. If we found, within the flexibility of controlling our own budget, that we were able to employ a full-time teacher to concentrate on children requiring additional support, I think we would be able to intervene at an earlier stage, before, it is hoped, the child has become disillusioned and lost enthusiasm for school. I do not wish to enter into a lengthy argument here about the pros and cons of special-school provision. We have some excellent special schools in Oxfordshire where children thrive and develop within the specialized approach appropriate to their needs. However, for the child experiencing difficulties with launching into their education and for whom there is no fundamentally apparent handicap (physical or mental) then, given adequate staffing provision, I think mainstream schools have much to offer.

RELATIONSHIPS WITH STAFF

I hope it will be apparent from my account that I consider all the staff in the school as a team, working together for the benefit of the children. Eight members of the teaching staff and two classroom assistants have been at St Andrew's for a considerable time and have experienced working under the direction of four headteachers – a volatile environment into which to introduce change, one might think. It did not prove to be so. When I arrived everyone was looking for some changes to be introduced. That is not to say that I didn't have to select developments with sensitivity, nor that all the new ideas I introduced were welcomed without question. But on the whole we are moving forward together with shared aspirations. I have appointed three teachers in the last three years, along with new and additional appointments of classroom and welfare assistants, lunchtime supervisors and, most recently, the caretaker. When considering applications I like to encourage people to visit prior to interview. In this way I hope to receive applications from those who feel they will be happy working alongside us. Opportunities to meet staff, formally and informally, also provide a guideline towards the possible blend of personalities. Experience has taught me that, no matter how rigorous I've tried to be, I've made a number of inappropriate appointments because none of us show our true selves until we are actually working in the school. I have been fortunate, however, to work in, and to lead schools where staff have worked together conscientiously, co-operatively and happily.

Miriam Wilcock

STAFF DEVELOPMENT

Having experienced the benefits of encouragement and challenge from senior personnel in education, I have always been concerned that individual members of staff have opportunities to extend and develop their personal skills and interests. The organization of a school offers many possibilities for individuals to be given a range of responsibilities. The deputy head no longer carries the role of a team co-ordinator – that position provides another member of staff the opportunity to augment their expertise. The 'A' incentive posts can be offered for short-term commitments, allowing me to invite staff with specific skills to share those with us and broaden their own professionalism. Teachers have always given generously of their time to fulfil roles of responsibility entrusted to them. But heads, unlike counterparts in industry, have not been able financially to reward these endeavours. Within the scope of a devolved budget it would appear that these circumstances might change, but I suspect it will be several years before we feel sufficiently comptent with this unfamiliar responsibility to be able to do more than follow the established patterns of remuneration.

For the last decade Oxfordshire has offered full support to teachers seeking to enhance their personal development. Three members of staff are pursuing M Ed qualifications in their own time, the fees and some release being met by the authority. Two teachers have received twenty-day secondments on consultancy courses in science and music during the year of writing. I have a member of staff on a half-day-a-week release to develop our strategies in assessment, profiling and record-keeping. The deputy head spent a day a week last year sharing her skills in the approach to drama with children at a local college of education. In the last two years staff have been involved in a joint secondment project with a partner secondary school, exploring ways in which liaison and continuity might be improved. During the last year, seven of us have attended training sessions offered by the authority on the implementation of National Curriculum stages 1 and 2 in the core subjects and in design and information technology, and the implementation of LMS. We have also taken advantage of courses offered by other institutions, in and outside Oxfordshire, utilizing our in-service allocation.

This level of in-service opportunity clearly benefits both staff and children, but there are some problems too. Supply staff are in heavy demand when county courses are arranged for schools in the same locality. Our regular team of supply teachers is being called upon by more schools, providing them with continuous employment. Teachers are feeling both anxious and guilty at the amount of time they are away from their own classes. Whenever someone has received fresh stimuli or training we like to be able to create time for this to be shared with us all. We have had great difficulty in consistently achieving this. The designated professional training days offer precious space for us to address some of our needs, and our difficulty is one of prioritizing. We become frustrated with the dilemma of knowing the value of in-service training and fulfilling our commitments in the classroom. Parents are confused and at times angry because they see the continuity of education for their children interrupted. In an attempt to respond to parental anxieties we invite governors, particularly parent governors, or any parent, to join us during a day's training and to judge for themselves the value of the day. Those who have taken up our offer continue to do much to 'evangelize' for us.

Despite all the perplexities I know that, if teachers are to grow and move forward in the profession, responsibility and continual training is essential for us all. In the last five years (straddling my previous as well as my current headship), I have had the satisfaction of seeing three members of staff move into headship and five move on to deputy headships.

We know from our initial training that children's motivation is fuelled when their efforts and achievements are acknowledged and praised. The same is equally true of adults and I place high priority on capitalizing on any opportunity that arises to compliment staff on their achievements, whether it is to the caretaker for clearing the weed from the pond, the secretary for reminding me to renew a subscription, a teacher's stimulating display or a training presentation at a staff meeting or training day. I place considerable value on 'thank yous', which represent the giving of that precious commodity, time. I try to ensure that any efforts given to the school by children, parents, governors or staff receive a personal note of gratitude from me, in addition to any verbal thanks I give.

PARENTAL INVOLVEMENT

I have already indicated some ways in which we attempt to involve parents as co-educators in the education of their children. Other ways in which we encourage parents to feel valued is to welcome them into school to work alongside us. Parents are frequently found in classrooms engaged in a variety of ways. They may be working with a group of children, passing on their own skills in craft, art, music or drama. They may be interacting with a group using the computer, following a research project in the library, engaged in some problem-solving activity set by the teacher or they may be listening and talking to children reading. The manner in which any teacher uses parents is an individual one. Some parents will work in the classes of their own children, others will work with teachers who don't have their children at the time.

Parent–teacher interviews are held at least twice a year but parents know, and take advantage of the fact, that they can come to talk to teachers or myself at any time. We aim to have one or two open mornings when all members of the community are encouraged to come to see us in action. We have four parent governors who act rigorously on behalf of the parents and the school to become involved and informed. Many parents offer their time to accompany us on day and residential visits and with follow-up work. Four parents hold county mini-bus driving licences, which enables them to assist with transport. The school association is well supported and actively engaged in organizing fund-raising events, approximately twice termly, re-alizing several thousands of pounds annually. I like to maintain an 'open-door' policy and attempt to be available to parents whenever and for whatever they feel a need to talk. They may arrange an appointment any time from 8 a.m. to 8 p.m. to discuss their children or their personal prob-lems. I don't guarantee any answers but I am prepared to offer a listening and sympathetic ear.

GOVERNORS

Our governing body now numbers 16 and is playing an increasingly influen-tial role in the life of the school. All governors attempt to participate in school activities as often as other commitments permit, which, on the whole, is not as frequently as they would like. Training sessions offered by the authority have provided valuable insight and directives towards the expected role of a governor in the nineties. We have established sub-groups to oversee finances, curriculum, staffing and premises. These groups are developing strategies to fulfil their terms of reference and I am con-fident that we shall meet the demands of ERA to the benefit of the school. I value the support and encouragement I receive from them all and look upon them as both colleagues and friends.

I became a teacher because I wanted to work with children and I have remained in school because it is from the children that I receive the great-est sense of job satisfaction. When I accepted the headship of a large school I was determined to try to get to know all 400 of them. I timetable myself into classes for one whole day a week. On this day I release those staff who have responsibilities to provide them with the opportunity to fulfil their role. I take a further four teaching sessions with other classes. I've found that I can get to more classes if I block my time, spending 5 or 6 weeks in one class then moving on to another group. My activities with any class will vary. I may continue with work already initiated. In a single session I might take some aspect of physical education, craft skill or handwriting, preparation or follow-up work related to an outside visit or recent experience. These are my objectives but there have been many occasions when my programme has been interrupted by commitments to county representation on a range of groups, by training for myself or providing an input to others and, more recently, in having to cover for absentee staff. My indulgence also puts heavy demands on my highly competent secretary who is left to deal with unexpected telephone calls or visitors (parents are notified of the day in the week when I am teaching full time). If she were not so efficient I would not feel able to take on this commitment. On the rare occasion when a response from me cannot wait, she or a classroom assistant will remain in a class. This is a common problem for the many full-time teaching heads in Oxfordshire.

I realize I am blessed with an efficient and experienced secretary and I try hard to ensure that I spend sufficient time during the week working alongside her. There are weeks when the administration runs smoothly and I feel that I am on target but, with the plethora of paperwork that has come through the door in recent months, the box of items still requiring attention grows ever larger.

One of my most frustrating and least enjoyable tasks is having to say no to requests, from staff or children, because of lack of financial resources. We benefit enormously from the generosity of our community but classrooms and libraries still need more books, we still do not have a computer in each classroom, we would like to incorporate a wider range of media into practical skills – to name but a few of our aspirations. We have learned to prioritize and be patient until we can afford the next item on the list.

Changes I think would help to minimize the level of stress I observe in all those who work in school are concerned with staffing. I would like to employ a full-time classroom assistant in every class and to have at least one full-time, permanent, member of staff over and above the number of classteachers required. I see the role of this person as being able to release others in blocks of time to enable us all realistically to meet our school-based responsibilities. As a fully involved and committed member of staff, this individual would be well placed to cover more effectively for staff away on personal development courses. I look forward optimistically, with the delegation of finances, to going some way towards achieving these aims. I think there have to be realistic levels of staffing at all stages of education so that personal links can be established and maintained as children move from one educational establishment to another. Detailed records and profiles offer invaluable information but cannot replace direct contact with personnel.

At St Andrew's the one change that would make my role as head more manageable would be to link the buildings as one. Sadly, I don't think this is achievable. To be relieved of a large part of the administration by appointing a bursar would also enable me to spend more of my time with staff and children. This would help me to achieve my own goals as a head-*teacher*. Perhaps this will also prove feasible under local financial management.

PERSONAL REFLECTIONS

As I reflect on ten years of headship, in two schools, I realize how fortunate I have been to be granted the opportunity to lead teams of such dedicated teachers. Their willingness to put into practice theories and ideas emanating from my experience fills me with humility. It has been a privilege to nurture and encourage the skills and talents of colleagues and enable them to accept wider responsibilities.

Our success as teachers is dependent upon the children in our care. The children are the heart of the school and it is they who give me a continual sense of excitement and challenge. One of the disadvantages of my room not being in the building with the classes of the youngest children is that it is not easy for them to trot in and out to me to share their achievements. I spend as much time as I am able drifting in and out of their rooms and am always inundated with requests to look at, or join in, ongoing work. One of my concerns is that we honestly see ourselves as a whole school and not as several, separate parts. To this end I place a great deal of emphasis on the place and value of our weekly whole-school assembly. It is the time when everyone is together. We celebrate successes and achievements within a planned and prepared half hour of praise and thanksgiving. This is not a time for reprimands or mundane notices. I want my influence on the gathered group to be positive and purposeful and this is handsomely repaid with their response and participation.

In conclusion, I must acknowledge the benefits I have received from the management training opportunities in Oxfordshire. This aspect of training is essential for those aspiring to headship. If schools are to become true places of excellence for all those working within them, management training should become the prerequisite of any senior post of responsibility. I have always held very high expectations of myself and of those with whom I work, children and adults, and imagine I might be seen as a hard taskmaster. My experience leads me to endorse that high expectations are the forerunner of high self-esteem and achievement. I see each day as a clean sheet of paper that may become filled with frenetic lines and symbols or may develop into something of lasting quality or form. Whatever it is, I hope to rest at the end of the day in the knowledge that I've given my best to the task.

Commentary

Like Morton (Chapter 3), Wilcock is concerned to raise children's self-esteem by providing the kind of purposeful, stimulating and caring environment that fosters good work but that also provides pupils with the security in which to experience and learn from failure. The speed at which ERA has been implemented, especially in LMS, has forced Wilcock and her colleagues to learn as they go along: not, as she points out, the 'best recipe for confidence building'.

Wilcock stresses the value of teachers developing their own individual styles of working but acknowledges that this welcome and natural diversity needs to be underpinned by the security of agreed policies. While placing a high priority on staff development and in-service work, Wilcock recognizes, as do many parents, the dilemma of staff involved in in-service training being away from classes and disrupting the children's continuity of education.

5
Pat Jones
Ysgol Gymraeg Castell-nedd

Pat Jones gained a teaching diploma slanted towards teaching in the Welsh language medium. She spent twelve years as a primary schoolteacher, during which she studied for a management diploma. After being a deputy head for three years, she was appointed to her current headship in 1984.

THE SCHOOL

Ysgol Gymraeg Castell-nedd lies in the heart of the community of Neath, in West Glamorgan. The town's community extends to numerous suburbs and the school's catchment area is wide. Over the years the site has housed three schools. Today there are two separate schools on the site, ours being one of them. The red-brick building, built in 1914, houses the main body of the school population (320 children). This building has a hall, six class-rooms, a staff-room (used also as a resources centre) and a headteacher's room. In addition to this main building, there are two Portacabins (pre-fabricated buildings housing three classes, added during the past five years to cope with an increasing school population) and, in a terraced house adjacent to the school, a nursery unit.

Neath is a bustling market town rich in environmental resources, on which we draw heavily. It has the remains of a Roman fort, a Norman castle and architectural features encompassing many historical periods. Adjacent to the school's site are leisure activities (swimming, tennis, playing fields), which we can also enjoy.

Ysgol Gymraeg Castell-nedd is a Welsh-medium school, which means that we offer parents the opportunity to educate their children through the medium of the Welsh language. The children who attend the school are there through parental choice – a conscious, conscientious choice. We offer them sound primary practice through the medium of Welsh. This choice must be supported by parents, and this is something we ask of parents when they come to the school to register their child. These parents are usually English speaking but they have decided to give their children the opportunity to be bilingual. I would estimate that 85 per cent of the children in the school come from English-speaking homes. These are Welsh families who only speak English. A small proportion, possibly 5 per cent of the whole, come from English families who do not speak Welsh.

Children are accepted into our nursery class at 3 years. They come on a part-time basis (spending either a morning or afternoon at school each day). Our aim is to make these children fluent in Welsh as soon as possible, and the method used is one of total immersion in the Welsh language. Many of these children have already been in Welsh-medium pre-school playgroups, and are acquainted with the language in a social context. Within this immersion programme, all instruction is in the second language, and the first language (English) is rarely used in the children's hearing. During the initial period at school, children use their mother tongue until they are able to use the second language. In Welsh-medium schools we are Welsh-speaking communities: pupils are encouraged and urged to interact and communicate in Welsh and so participate in class activities. Children assimilate and acquire the language quickly and easily, and by the age of 16 are as able to sit the same Welsh-medium examinations as their peers from Welsh-speaking homes.

Parents chose our schools for a variety of reasons. Some wish their children to acquire a second language, and research has shown that bilingualism can enhance intellectual and educational activities. There are those who feel they want their children to be able to live a full and meaningful existence within their own country, and the acquisition of one's national language can only serve to foster a feeling of belonging and an appreciation of the heritage of their country.

Teachers use English only infrequently. During the children's period in the nursery there is a constant assimilation of the language, and the confidence to use the language, naturally, will vary from individual to individual. There are also children in these classes whose first language is Welsh and these form a valuable linguistic resource for their peer group. The children's oral fluency is assessed by their comprehension of what is being said to them, as shown in their response to it. This initial fluency is apparent in the reception class, but teachers are aware of their vital role in ensuring and reinforcing language growth. We find the system of total immersion vindicated since children do not leave for local English-medium schools very often. As in all schools, children do choose to leave, but not normally on linguistic grounds. If they do leave on these grounds, parents tend to believe that their lack of educational progress is associated with a bilingual education, a supposition that has not been proved. Conversely, parents of children in English-medium schools have transferred their children to us at 9 years and, because of a centre for 'late-comers' that was set up at our Welsh-medium comprehensive school, these children are able to attend the centre for three days a week for two school terms to learn the language. Again, the method of teaching the language is through total immersion, and those children after two terms are able to cope within our classrooms with Welsh teaching. These centres were initially set up to enable the children of English families who came to Wales to live to be educated in Welsh at their local primary schools. The success of these centres has been most encouraging.

My initial training was geared towards teaching in Welsh-medium schools and I have spent my entire career in them. But to begin at the beginning. After twelve years in various primary classrooms, feeling reasonably satisfied with my lot, exploring various approaches and techniques, listening to differing theories and philosophies, one day came the question, 'Have you thought about applying to become a member of the new management course at the West Glamorgan Institute of Higher Education?' This question, which came from a particularly supportive primary adviser, provoked a period of self-questioning. Did I really want a year away from the classroom as part of a course designed for the personal and professional development of primary schoolteachers who were looking for positions of senior management in schools? No, I did not think so. I had not thought of management outside the classroom. Then, I thought, why not? Subsequently, the following September, I was a member of the primary management course. This gave me a year away from the classroom, a year of discourse, of rethinking and deciding what education was really about. I could look at things from the outside, from a different perspective. I could question and re-evaluate. For example, on a visit to a primary school in Dorset, I encountered for the first time such superb primary practice that it influenced my entire thinking and, indeed, my subsequent career. Yes, it was possible to translate theory into practice. The school exuded quality and the excitement of children learning. After this, I knew I would like to try it for myself.

Four years later I was given the opportunity, the challenge I had been waiting for. I was appointed headteacher of Ysgol Gymraeg Castell-nedd. September 1984 was the beginning. Armed with my experience of classroom practice and a revitalized philosophy, I took up the gauntlet thrown before me. I clearly remember the first day of being headteacher. I wondered where I should begin – I had been told so many times on the management course, 'Don't change too many things at first'. The question was, which things should come first?

In my initial report to the governors of the school, I wrote

> certainly as a new head, the task of accomplishing certain aims within the school will take time and I will be reporting on each development regarding school policy and curriculum development at future meetings. The first term has been one in which I have attempted to improve the fabric of the building.

At the outset, my assessment was that standards needed to rise, standards of learning, of teaching and of the school premises. All aspects within the school needed looking at, and so I had to set priorities and the decision I made at the time was

1. we needed to improve the standard and condition of the fabric of the school and its environs; and
2. we needed an on-going programme of staff development.

These would be the foundations for growth. But these were not tasks that could be accomplished overnight. They needed the co-operation and commitment of every member of staff. They needed team effort. Any development depended totally on the staff team, on their co-operation and commitment, on a professional attitude towards the achievement of the task we were being paid to do.

During the early months (and subsequently the early years) the plan began to take shape. A walk around the school with the chairman of governors during the first week initiated the support that brought vital improvements to the fabric – a new roof, re-wiring, internal repairs and redecoration of the school took almost two years of upheaval.

When the programme of staff development had been set in motion it began with looking at scale-post allowances, which had been allocated before my appointment but not as I wanted them. I decided that I would redefine them. Changes of responsibilities were made. I saw it my role to develop the staff's teaching skills, for which they would need the training provided by LEA courses (sometimes involving a term's secondment). Further training included the observation of good practice in other schools, and discussion and planning as a team. I found that individual interviews with members of staff were both informative and useful in this training programme. These interviews have continued throughout the years. I think a more formal, recorded response to these interviews should now be initiated at the school: this is a current project.

PERSONAL PHILOSOPHY OF EDUCATION

If I have a personal philosophy of education it is that children pass through primary school just once and, as educators, we must ensure that this passage is a successful one. Education must be about the success of the individual. It is a very special responsibility we undertake and we need every professional skill available to us. We need clear thinking, sound planning and good management.

I believe that the education we provide is very much a matter of critical decisions and judgements. We need to question and to justify our work. If we cannot do this, then our task and efforts mean nothing. Education is the process by which we hope to develop our children into adults, equipped with the necessary tools for the life they have to lead. Children are unique individuals, each with his or her own special talent that we need to discover, nurture and develop – not an easy task but, being aware of the differences, a school must aim to provide for, and cope with, every child. Education should not be equated with academic achievement: the artistic or athletic child is as important as the talented academic. We need to capitalize on each child's strength and, through it, make him or her successful. Language is the pivot for all the activities within the school.

I believe schools should, at all times, reflect quality. The environment for learning should reflect quality and create an ethos that will enable children to relate to the school and its community and promote a sense of belonging for them. The quality of teaching practice must recognize the levels of skills and abilities of individual children and enable the individual teacher to respond positively to the needs of the children and enable them to experience success. We need to engender a quality of confidence among all people involved with the school to demonstrate their commitment and support to the ideals of the school.

ORGANIZATION AND MANAGEMENT OF LEARNING

In order to put such a philosophy into practice, there needed to be a team aiming for the same goals. As a new head, I had to build this team. Would the participants want innovation, and the responsibility innovation brings?

I suppose the first reaction was one of low morale and resistance to the requirements of change. Establishing a team committed to the same goals is not easy.

Formulating goals, although it appears to be a result of consensus, is not always so. One may have an amalgam, but not a consensus. Members of the team can be unsure and silently avoid the translation of goals into practice through non-cooperation. In this situation, one must try to ensure that the majority sets the pace and standards, and the minority remains just that – a minority. A team directed to a specific goal must be involved in discussion: ideas and projects shared are a source of encouragement.

To establish a team committed to a set of goals was my priority. But prejudices and preconceived antagonism made it a difficult task. The frustration of counter objectives, lack of understanding, unwillingness to agree, all blocked the path to achieving accord. But there was also support and encouragement. It came from the school's primary adviser and from members of staff who were willing to try for the first time an experimental approach to curriculum development. I went with a classteacher and children on a visit to the castle and, together, we were able to explore the possibilities the ruins brought. There was a positive response from a colleague who had not previously approached learning and teaching in this way. Classrooms began, slowly, to reflect quality.

I was fortunate in being able to obtain new classroom furniture (through the support of the advisory service). This made an enormous difference to classroom organization because it influenced teaching styles. Desks and pupils had been static, but the new tables and units encouraged flexibility and movement. Trolleys for equipment meant that resources were more readily accessible. The school had been repainted and classrooms presented an improved quality of environment. Children's work was better displayed. These improvements did not impress all: headteachers must be aware that not everyone thinks such matters have anything to do with education. I have learnt not to be daunted but to carry on with the plan.

I found deeply entrenched academic values among the staff. There must be pen-on-paper tasks and 80-per-cent success before 'good' has anything to do with education. Management, organization, planning and evaluation have an uphill job to change this. There will continue to be those who believe that education is solely about academic success and has nothing to do with qualities developed for living in the real world.

When one is dealing with narrowly focused values, and when lip service is being paid to developments, one needs drive and determination to overcome the effects of those attitudes. The monitoring of developments is a rewarding facet of the job. I have found that the monitoring process is best carried out by looking at children's work together as a team, by joint discussion on specific topics and by holding team meetings in alternating classrooms. This enables individual teachers to tell us all about their particular theme, the work that has emanated from it and the difficulties or the successes they have had. Obviously, the skills of individual teachers vary, but those who are able to share enrich the curriculum.

We have tried different approaches to develop skills we have agreed are important for the whole school. We decided, for example, that potato printing was a skill we wanted to use throughout the school. It was important as a pre-reading skill in the left-to-right progression from line to line and it could be developed to a point of excellence with the refining of pattern aiding mathematical accuracy. We could use the skill throughout the age-ranges and use the patterns produced in book-making activities and for a variety of display purposes. A teacher led the initial training session and from this the practice was assimilated into the different classrooms. Development of this skill was a joint, agreed objective that involved the whole school through staff-led initiative and sharing.

Watching children learn is, perhaps, the most rewarding of experiences and one feels privileged in being able to see this happen. A walk through the school shows a host of activities taking place and a teacher may invite one to share in an activity or to suggest a way forward.

How are teaching weaknesses remedied? Methods vary – by training, by the example of teacher colleagues, by discussion – but actually changing practice is far more complicated. I feel the answer must lie with a vision of the requirements needed to enable children to experience success, and by a sound understanding of the development of children. Part of this vision must surely include the quality of support a child needs to encapsulate the wholeness of his or her education. Whatever the issue under review, we must of necessity come back to teacher interest and commitment. Without these two elements, nothing can be developed, and teachers and children are so much the poorer.

We organize the school around the development of curriculum areas allocated to those teachers competent or interested and committed to various subject areas. The objectives emanating from the main aims for the school are agreed by a staff team for each subject/curriculum area and from these class teachers are able to develop flow charts illustrating a thematic approach to the curriculum. Within this structure, teachers are able to monitor the learning pattern of individual children. Teachers are discouraged from interrupting the learning process by following a tightly structured group approach to teaching, which is too rigidly linked to time. I feel it is important to allow children to have time to complete tasks. Children often have to struggle against time 'targets' or 'key stages'. There can often be a battle against time. Why shouldn't tasks be completed without being curtailed by the time factor? I realize that this is a highly individualistic approach, and for it to take place within classes, the teacher must be totally confident and experienced so that the needs and activities of the rest of the class are catered for too. It requires a discipline within the class, a self-discipline among the children, so that each class member can spend time on tasks and complete them. Such flexibility as this will be affected by the National Curriculum. Activities and tasks will be restricted and confined if teachers consider the pressures of increased attainment targets for numerous subjects as uppermost in the decisions they have to make as to what children should or shouldn't be engaged in doing or learning. When teachers consider how little can be done in a day, the enormity of the task that faces them and the recording of the assessment they need to keep on each child are tremendous pressures.

In our school, teachers meet on a weekly basis to monitor their programmes and progress (and to discuss any problems they may individually have experienced during the week) with a view to sharing difficulties or developments. As a team we find these sessions a source of support and, recently, in the field of design and technology, a way forward. This was an area in which the staff felt somewhat unsure, but through discussion and a practical sharing of classroom projects, much success and progress has been achieved in a comparatively short space of time. It is refreshing to sit around a table and look at children's work: this is real assessment of teacher and child. It helps identify the strengths that exist within the school and, equally, the weaknesses.

Curriculum development should have been a high priority for a new head. It could have headed the list. However, the reality of the situation was that it was not possible to take over the school and develop the curriculum overnight. I remember speaking to my primary adviser, as I did frequently in those difficult early days, and expressing my sentiments regarding this development: it was something that would have to come later. I was fortunate in the support I received from him, the regular visit to a new head, and the encouragement that spurred me on. This is what the new head needs.

Later on, having accomplished the initial strategy, I saw the advisory service as an integral part of the development of specific areas of the curriculum. The work we were doing needed to be seen in the context of current practice. An example of this occurred in mathematics. The mathematics adviser agreed to assess the current situation. He visited every class, monitored and suggested ways forward. Teachers were encouraged to be involved in discussions and, at the end of the programme, the school and staff benefited enormously. Our mathematics adviser became a regular visitor to the school over a period of time. After-school meetings were arranged and, as headteacher, I was able to plan future development.

This kind of response from the advisory service is positive, but I have also experienced the reverse. I asked for expertise in a curriculum area where a teacher and her class were at a specific developmental point and needed immediate advice (which, in my view, would only have taken a little time). The response this time was negative and help was deferred to the next term. The following term help was further deferred. The staff and I felt no response was available to meet their immediate needs.

To return to the mathematics development programme, it certainly helped team-building in the school: from this particular exercise a whole-school policy has been developed and there has been a steady implementation of the suggestions made at the time.

These difficult, early days were mainly during my first year as head-teacher, in my transition from being a classteacher to a completely different role of being responsible for a whole school. The adjustment, I suppose, is similar for most and advice is given from many sources. There was pressure to make the right decisions and to answer criticisms.

TIMES OF CHANGE

This was the mid-1980s and there were rumblings of a National Curriculum and its associated requirements. We needed confirmation and reassurance of what we were doing. Our teachers felt under threat and their morale was low. Was this new curriculum going to undermine the child-centred approach to the development of the curriculum? Therefore, when the opportunity arose to submit the school for the Curriculum Award of the School Education Officers, it seemed an ideal opportunity to seek affirmation that the approach we had was sound, and the curriculum we were developing was relevant. The outlined philosophy and idea of the award seemed credible: 'the processes of education are as important as the content . . . and . . the ethos of the school is itself an educational force'. This was certainly something that concurred with the notion of success and quality. Staff morale needed boosting: perhaps this was another opportunity for an exercise in staff development. Morale seems to be low when changes are imminent, when people feel threatened and are unable to cope with them. Staff development had to be about an endorsement of the fact that the practice we were trying to ensure for the children in our care was sound. I felt the staff deserved to be told that they must build on the foundation we were trying to secure. We needed national recognition of this.

Our submission for the curriculum award was accepted, and during the year the school was visited by national assessors. Eventually we were told of our success in the award. Representatives of the governing body, some pupils and myself visited London to receive the award. It was certainly a worthwhile exercise because of the boost it gave to staff.

However, the National Curriculum had not gone away. In my view, it had come about because of the perception that there was under-achievement in British schools. Was the great education debate founded on a false premiss? Whether or not this was true, it was thought necessary to produce a National Curriculum that would raise standards. At present, we do not feel that the National Curriculum is enhancing children's education. Rather, a situation has arisen whereby teachers are requested to ensure that thousands of statements of achievement are presented to hundreds of children, an assessment made and a record kept of progress. Children are not that easily defined and teachers are finding difficulties in reconciling their child-centred approaches with the subject-centred approach of the National Curriculum. In fact, some of my staff feel the two are not reconcilable.

In spite of many doubts or protests that may have been raised, the rumours of a National Curriculum were soon followed by confirmation in the form of documents – mathematics and science initially – and from that point onwards we have been bombarded with more and more reading material. As a head, I felt immediately that the initial reaction from teach-ers was one of panic. What did all this mean for their current practice? The answer I gave was, if our educational philosophy was sound, and was based on the way children learn, then this philosophy could assimilate any new curriculum. The message for teachers was that they must continue to work in the same way. We now doubt if this will be possible – philosophies regarding children learning on the one hand – and knowledge of subject assimilated on the other are difficult to reconcile.

As head, I attended meetings of clarification and elucidation on National Curriculum documents. Many of them seemed to be forgetting the child; there was an emphasis on subjects. The philosophy behind the National Curriculum seemed to take over the notion of the child being central, and individual needs being catered for through an appreciation of personality as well as ability. In the classrooms, teachers have to come to terms with statutory requirements gradually assuming paramount importance, al-though this is not what we would want. Our whole-school curriculum is crucial to us. We have worked hard to develop a curriculum that caters for

the child and his or her needs, and now themes and topics are being geared
to predetermined statutory requirements.

I feel we have to remind teachers about the *child*. We plan, then refer to
legislation afterwards. We are still looking for ways in which we can secure
the best of the planning system we previously had and fulfil the requirements of the National Curriculum. It is not easy.

Don't forget the child and his or her education. This had to be a clear
message to all teachers from a headteacher. We must not forget our philosophy. The new National Curriculum guidelines carried paradoxical
messages, because they wanted the best of both worlds. They demanded a
structured subject approach, and yet talked of cross-curricular approaches
as well. We have yet to consolidate the two: so far we find that it's not
possible.

We heard of cross-curricular assessment (or testing). SATs began to be
an everyday term – dreaded and feared. We knew that we already assessed
children, it was an integral part of the teachers' work, and a relevant one.
We were chosen to be a pilot school for one of the SATs consortia. (The
consortia were anxious to use Welsh-medium schools like ours.) It trans-
pired that SATs were time-consuming, taking valuable teaching time, and
our verdict at the end was that we knew no more about the children than
we had known previously. It was an unnecessary exercise with no direct
benefit to the children's education, and the feedback confirmed what we
had assessed already.

I feel the whole question of external 'assessment' has been one aspect
teachers have been informed least about, because no one seems to be
giving direct, decisive information. Teachers do not know *how* they should,
what they should or *when* they should assess in accordance with the National Curriculum. As headteachers we are called to meetings where, in my
view, the woolly statements being offered – 'Don't panic', 'Don't worry'
and consolations regarding SATs: 'They're not as bad as we feared' – are
certainly not what we need to hear. We are not in a profession where such
compromises can be acceptable; we have precious little time to educate the
children in our care. Teachers need to hear positive statements and to be
encouraged to do their job as they know how to do it best. As a head, I
have felt that everyone is fumbling in the dark on this issue.

The years 1989–90 have been difficult for teachers. They have been
bombarded with reading material from all directions, and to make sense of
it, to maintain a philosophy and to keep up with the daily round of teaching
activity, has been quite a feat. Within our own LEA the production of a
policy statement for the curriculum was essential, because it contains sensible guidelines we can follow, which are relevant to the kind of schools and

the mode of education we are attempting to achieve. This policy statement emerged as the result of extensive discussions involving elected members, officers, headteachers, parents, teachers, industrialists and trade-union representatives within West Glamorgan. It is intended to provide a constructive overview of the curriculum within the county and a clear statement of the objectives that should underpin the work of every school. This local curriculum encompasses the National Curriculum.

Following the initial document, which outlines the basic principles, aims and ethos individual establishments would have, and how the processes of teaching and learning, assessment and organization should be approached, the authority has provided schools with comprehensive guides (*Primary Curriculum in Practice*) to the implementation of this policy in the various areas of experience – early years, home–school links, empirical experiences (discovery work), the expressive arts, and so on. The statement of policy for the authority has been particularly valuable for schools that are trying actively to protect and conserve those things they know to be valuable. It is concerned with process rather than content, with a variety of teaching styles and with effective ways of transmitting the curriculum. We have reminders of the dangers of putting back the clock of progress in the process of education and avoiding an over-concentration on content, as prescribed by the National Curriculum. There are positive statements of the National Curriculum being taught in relation to the local curriculum, which is endorsed by the governors of individual schools.

GOVERNORS

Apart from the National Curriculum, the Education Reform Act 1988 (ERA) set about extending the powers of governors and pointed in the direction of local management of schools (LMS). My approach to the governing body aimed to achieve a partnership with this group. Governors need to be able to make decisions about a school based on the confidence they have in the professionalism of the staff they employ in the school.

We have twelve governors, a group formed in accordance with the requirements laid down by ERA. I sought to influence the composition of lay members of the group and to attract people with an interest in the philosophy and aims of the school. On this basis we were successful in appointing a local solicitor, a founder-parent of the school and a national sporting personality, all of whom have extended the influence of the school into the community through their professional and social contacts.

Governors meet at least once a term, when I report to them. They are invited to participate in the major events in the school calendar and are a valuable link between school and community. The diversity of opinion that exists generates healthy discussion, especially in terms of the financial priorities of the school. Because of the composition of the group, I have been fortunate in having available the expert resource of a professional accountant (co-opted as an LEA governor) whose advice is invaluable in areas of management in which I have little personal expertise, such as finance. The knowledge I am gaining from these people is of particular value to the school.

The relationship between the head and governors is a delicate balance whereby the group and the head must develop a mutual trust and understanding of the requirements of the school, while taking account of the philosophy, thoughts and ideas of individual members. However, because of the requirements of ERA and the responsibilities placed upon lay people, there is a challenge to achieve, on behalf of the school, the best possible provision.

LOCAL MANAGEMENT OF SCHOOLS

As a consequence of the pending introduction of LMS, we agreed, as a school, to bcome participants in a pilot scheme run by the LEA. This began in April 1987 and involved sixteen primary schools. I felt our participation would be a gain for the school. It was felt that we were competent to make decisions and that the scheme would facilitate decision-making at a local level. In reality, it also involved the competence of the governors to administer the scheme and decide on priorities. To date, we have become accustomed to the constraints of the scheme and, though not yet fully delegated, we have a pretty clear idea of the financial and political restrictions on manoeuvrability due to regulations and lack of funding.

At the beginning, we had problems in co-ordinating information. Anomalies arose and it was difficult to plan because we did not have a complete picture. Meters – gas, water, electricity – took on a new importance: they had to be seen to and read. This was not easy as costs had to be apportioned with another school on the same site. It is extremely difficult to have a degree of accuracy in this situation.

The headteacher's room, plus clerk's desk, has been filled with new equipment. Monitors, keyboard and printers arrived but we did not and still do not have appropriate furniture to house them. New equipment meant training and here there has been a planned programme by the LEA. On the positive side, because of an increased pupil roll, I was fortunate in being able to increase the school clerk's hours and ensure that she was trained, because I could not guarantee that my school day would be spent becoming familiar with the new computer system.

Headteacher colleagues have been seconded by the LEA to become consultants for LMS and they have played a crucial role in ensuring more adequate, relevant information for us. Primary support officers have also been employed (to provide clerical support from the centre) and they have a monitoring role, in so far as the budget is concerned. This allows the LEA to maintain an overview of the application of budgetary requirements in the school. We have been allocated a primary (clerical) support officer who visits us when required and attends governing-body meetings when invited. It seems reasonable to assume, however, that financial planning will become part of the necessary training and development programme for future headteachers. While the support of these officers is currently valuable, I envisage their influence will diminish as current and future headteachers acquire expertise in the accounting and financial planning requirements of their schools and the management of their budgets.

As headteacher, I welcomed the opportunity to participate. However, while the scheme was designed to give greater flexibility in decision-making and establishing priorities at the local base, the reality is that the budgets agreed by the LEA are not adequate to give the flexibility required. Further, we are at present restricted to seeking quotations from a centralized source that quotes prices that are highly inflated relative to the budget set. The full effect of LMS can only be evaluated after more experience has been gained in its application, and with the greater involvement of local governing bodies in budget preparations.

PARENTS

In addition to a partnership with governors, my vision for the school included partnership and involvement for parents in the educative process of the child. We need to inform parents of what we are trying to achieve and advise them on how they can help. In a successful school, with the education of children the primary aim, we require the co-operation of parents. I have tried to involve parents in all aspects of school life, as part of the partnership to promote the well-being of all children. However, to integrate parents successfully, there must be a recognition by the parents of the limits of their sphere of influence in the school. The parental role is a supportive one. The policy of the school is the responsibility of the governing body of the school and the application of the policy is the responsibility of the head and staff of the school. Parents can influence both the policy and its application by discussing their concerns, suggestions or complaints with the head or any member of the governing body of the school.

In a school such as ours parental links are strong. Support is forthcoming from people who have made a conscious choice of a particular form of education. There are positive home–school links. Parents have chosen Welsh-medium education for their children and sometimes want to know if this differs from the education given by other schools. They are assured that this is not so.

The vision that one has for a school is that there should be an openness about education, that a school cannot operate in isolation without the support of a community – a community that encompasses parents. Children are influenced in a variety of ways but, in my view, the three main forces of influence are home, school and community. If all three are striving towards the same end, we are well on our way towards achieving our goals. Ideally, the total commitment and support of the parents to the school's aims would mean that two of the three influences are pointed in the same direction and would be of tremendous value in the development of the third aspect.

As schools, we cannot be sure of parents' commitment, and so we have to remind parents constantly of the importance of their supportive role. As a profession we have a clear obligation to our parents. They have to be our allies. We consult them, confide in them and seek their co-operation. They can become involved in the daily life of the school, but this involvement is changing as so many of our parents are engaged in their own career progression and we find fewer who can regularly assist us in the education process. We have a number who are available and help in classrooms under teacher direction and a valuable few who enable us, through their commitment after school, to run a successful school orchestra and gymnastic club.

The school has a parents' association, which is committed to supporting the school. It forms a valuable extension to the involvement of parents by the promotion of social relationships among people with differing status in society, meeting together with a common purpose, i.e. to do whatever they can to promote the well-being of the school. Fund-raising is a part of their activities, but I have tried to emphasize a different role by arranging for specialist advisers to speak to them on educational matters and events that relate to the Welsh cultural ethos, which underpins the school.

PERSONAL REFLECTIONS

Frustrations of the job centre around the lack of external support services when required; having to accept, on behalf of the children, mediocrity in the support services not directly involved in classroom practice; being told that the SATs situation is acceptable when one's personal conviction is that it is not; and when one knows that, at LEA level, there is a diversity of opinion that confuses the issue still further.

Change that might enhance the profession would be a closer involvement of teachers in the initial training programme and a stronger liaison with the training institutions. In the training years the basic concepts regarding the education of children must be nurtured and understood. It would be helpful, too, if central government recognized that the education of children is not cheap and requires adequate resources. The emphasis on, and resources devoted to, the development of assessment procedures, which add no value to the education process in the early years, might be better spent in other ways.

After six years of being a head I still look forward to the challenges and the difficult decisions each day brings. I don't feel under pressure except that my job necessitates planning, organization and decision-making that cover a wide variety of different aspects of school life. I value most the support I receive from my staff and the parents of the children who attend my school.

As one who has drawn great personal satisfaction from the profession I recommend that, if a head considers the child first and foremost in all aspects of the development of a school, he or she cannot fail to develop a successful school.

Commentary

Jones, in her Welsh-medium school, argues strongly for language immersion from the time children start school. She favours a thematic approach to the curriculum, with few constraints upon the time in which pupils are allowed to complete tasks. The advent of the National Curriculum, attainment targets and SATs will affect this flexibility – adversely, in Jones's view. She is critical of the National Curriculum, seeing it as a threat to the child-centred education philosophy and a cause of low teacher morale.

The concept of quality – of environment, of teaching and of confidence – is central to Jones's philosophy and, she maintains, needs for its attainment the support of a unified team, composed of interested and committed teachers. Jones's early experiences of managing change emphasize the importance of informed support for the head, from sources external to the school. As we have commented before, the role of a head can be lonely, particularly when he or she wishes to introduce unpopular changes. Like Morton (Chapter 3), Jones considers that governments should recognize that education needs adequate resourcing to maintain quality. Teacher involvement in initial teacher training, she argues, might help to instil and nurture at an early stage basic concepts of child education.

6
Marilyn Keerak
Sunningdale Elementary School

Marilyn Keerak was appointed principal of the new Sunningdale Elementary School, in Moose Jaw, Saskatchewan, Canada, in 1985. Prior to her appointment she had the opportunity to participate in the actual planning and design of the facility. Mrs Keerak holds a master of education degree from the University of Regina. Over the past twenty-five years, she has taught all levels of education: elementary, high school, university and advanced adult.

Marilyn Keerak is deeply concerned about the community in which she lives. Currently she serves on the Board of Directors of Diversified Services, a rehabilitation centre for the handicapped; she is provincial chairperson of the Girl Guides Water Project; she edits a journal for the Saskatchewan Reading Council; and she is involved in provincial and regional recreational and cultural programmes on a consultative basis. Mrs Keerak is married with three children.

THE SCHOOL

Sunningdale School is a twelve-classroom building. The single-storey structure has skylights and windows that allow greater environmental appreciation. In the summer, prairie grain crops can be observed ripening before the harvest. In the winter, harsh winds sweep snow and cold across the northerly expanse of the playground.

The school sits on the edge of the city's newest residential land development. Between the school and the bulk of the development is a 50-acre strip of public park, which is gradually being developed for recreation. The community and school board have jointly developed a large creative play-ground and plans for a grassed and irrigated playing field on two sides are now complete. The lovely green and brown colour tones in the building complement the rich browns and golds of the surrounding prairie landscape.

Pupils attending this school come from two city sub-divisions, a radius of up to two kilometres from the school site. There is a city bus available to the door of the school. In good weather, students prefer to use the paved bike path joining their sub-division to the school. Sunningdale is con-sidered to be one of the more affluent areas of the city. Most parents are employed in management or mid-management positions. Most students are European Canadian in origin and are Protestant. Fifteen European countries are represented in our school, the greater percentage of the population tracing its descent to Great Britain, although students are third or fourth generation Canadian. We have no treaty Indians in our popu-lation. Catholic children have the option of being bussed directly to a Roman Catholic school further in the more central part of the city.

Education is valued and supported by the community. Parents have good educational backgrounds and are specific in their expectations for their children. Parents are self-confident in dealing with school-related matters. They are also very willing to pursue their concerns with higher authorities either locally or provincially.

PERSONAL PHILOSOPHY OF EDUCATION

Sunningdale School might best be described as the product of a rather interesting 'Moose Jaw Experience'. In 1977 I travelled with two other educators to the campus at the University of California in Los Angeles to work with Dr Madeline Hunter for ten days. Those ten educationally packed days profoundly changed our directions in education.

Dr Hunter had developed a clinical-supervision approach to staff de-velopment and evaluation. Her work was based on what she considered to be the basics of education: motivation, retention, reinforcement, rate and degree of learning and transfer of learning. When these principles are used in combination with the elements of a good lesson, good teaching will occur. The principal must accept the role of instructional leader. Within the clinical-supervision model, the principal who is well versed in pedagogy coaches the teacher. The teacher brings to this partnership a good founda-tion of knowledge of the content in a particular subject area or at a particular grade level. Dr Hunter's words were inspirational. We quickly became converts to her philosophy of education, which was positive, humane and highly professional.

The three of us returned to Moose Jaw filled with missionary-like zeal. It was from these ten days that the 'Moose Jaw Experience' began. This experience formally spanned a decade and informally continues to shape much of the system's response even today.

In an effort to share our information in a more systematic way, we developed a team approach to in-service training. It was decided that, in order to keep the model pure and unaffected, the three of us would work together in each presentation. We developed a programme that involved initial observations of the teachers in their classrooms. Our role was to label the good things we observed. We then asked permission to use a few of these examples as part of our formal presentation. It took one, two-hour training session per week over a ten-week period. When we were finished, we hoped to leave each school with a positive way of looking at their efforts, and with a common vocabulary to use in their professional discussion. The principal then had a tool by which to supervise teachers so as to help them grow professionally, as well as an instrument to assist in the writing of formal evaluatory reports. Principals also received some additional in-service training.

That's the theory! In practice, while all ten elementary schools in our division did participate to some degree, the professional growth was interrupted by many extraneous factors, over which we had no control. Petty jealousies sprang up ('I'd talk up a pretty good story if I had my way paid to Los Angeles!'). Real fears made teachers feel insecure ('How can an ex-jock (the principal) really understand early childhood education?'). Reluctantly the team revised their initial plans. We decided to move more slowly and work with those people who seemed positive. The workshop package was styled 'More Effective Teaching'. Team members returned to Los Angeles for a further ten days of training. Dr Hunter spent ten days of her summer in Moose Jaw. My personal professional growth was truly enhanced.

I was now ready to try out these basic ideas in an accepting environment. When the principalship of a small inner-city-type school in the system became vacant we resolved to make it a pilot school. The questions we hoped to answer were as follows:

1. Is it important for the principal to be an instructional leader as well as an educational manager?
2. Do students learn better in a planned, positive, humane environment?
3. Can we effect positive educational change by concentrating on the basic components of pedagogy?

The project would be given two years before its final external evaluation. King Edward School was chosen as the pilot site and I was appointed principal. There was no vice-principal.

The staff at King Edward School were not so elated. All but two gave polite 'thanks but no thanks' to the invitation to be part of the project. It was to be expected. Educational change is slow to effect. We had still moved too quickly. We were not sufficiently conscious of public relations. We did not understand the power of parent and public involvement.

Eventually a complete staff of people committed to the project was trained and put in place. I personally was very grateful to our board of trustees, who believed in the project through the many days when the press chose to misunderstand our task. There was a constant barrage of negative press releases for the first two months of our existence. Although it quietened somewhat, even over the New Years Eve of our first pilot year, a negative comment appeared in the letters to the local editor.

Fortunately through all of this our belief in what we were doing was not shaken. I am convinced that it is very important to have one's belief structure firmly in place before undertaking any change. Without describing it in detail, it is sufficient to say that the project was successful. We did manage to raise both personal image and academic standards. There was evidence that the principal played an important role as the instructional leader. This did not appear to be hampered by the fact that the principal also wrote final evaluative reports on teachers.

Given that the school system had developed a clear statement of philosophy and subscribed to a system-wide set of goals, the climate made evaluation by principal supervision and school-based teacher professional development a real possibility. More effective teaching became the core around which this change took place.

As a result of these experiences, when I became principal of Sunningdale School, I had a very clear set of belief statements on which I wished to found this new school.

Belief No. One

The principal must be the instructional leader. This means being knowledgeable about current trends in educational pedagogy. It implies setting a role model of energy, industry and, above all, a willingness to learn. It is important that the principal attends conferences, visits other schools and networks with other administrators as often as possible so that the vision does not become drowned in the flood of paperwork that inevitably crosses one's desk. It is imperative that the principal be highly visible within classrooms, out in playgrounds, at school functions and within the community. The school principal cannot live isolated from either political or civic affairs: these too are a part of the fabric of education life. It is important, however, that the principal attempts to be above shallow bias and personal self-interest.

Belief No. Two

Administration is most effective as a team effort. While the principal holds the ultimate accountability and cannot relinquish this, there are still many areas where shared responsibility and shared ownership of leadership make for the operation of a more effective and cohesive unit. This team effort involves a close liaison with central office (local authority) personnel as well as compatibility with one's vice-principal. It involves accepting the fact that teachers, too, have professional dreams. The principal becomes a facilitator in the achievement of these ends. Staff then become stakeholders in the important decisions of the school.

Belief No. Three

Learning is an activity for students, staff and administrators. Staff need to be coached as they gain instructional insights. Administrators need coaching in the many roles they must play. All the learners in the school environment have distinctive learning styles. Fortunately, all will flourish in a positive and humane climate. It is important to catch staff and students doing things right and build on that base.

SCHOOL ORGANIZATION

Sunningdale School is a kindergarten to grade-eight school within Moose Jaw Public School Division No. 1. The policy of the division allows this school of 355 students to have a full-time principal and a vice-principal, who is scheduled one-quarter time for administrative duties. The school has one-and-a-half full-time para-professionals (welfare and clerical assistants) assigned for office duty, playground supervision and other clerical tasks.

The administrative team annually facilitates the setting of school priorities. These major objectives may be administrative decisions or a product of staff decision-making. The vice-principal and I meet formally on a weekly basis to set goals for the week. On a daily basis we share information and experiences in a more casual manner.

Using the duties as defined by the Saskatchewan Education Act as a basis, we must deal administratively with the following fifteen operations.

1. Attendance reporting   Attendance is not a problem at our school. Students are anxious to be there and attend regularly. We deliberately plan monthly school events over and above classroom events to enhance the positive feeling towards the school. We do have concerns, though, if students are absent and we monitor attendance daily to be aware of accident, truancy or abduction possibilities.

Daily attendance reporting is the responsibility of the teacher. However, the official attendance records are maintained by our office staff. This removes some of the clerical duties from the desk of the teacher. I feel strongly that this is necessary to free the professional to do what he or she does best – teach.

2. Budget monitoring   The budget for the school system comes from two sources. Approximately 39 per cent is provided through provincial government grants. Any additional funds come from a local tax levy and tuition fees from neighbouring school divisions as determined by the locally elected board of trustees. Funds are allocated to the schools on the basis of per-pupil grants. At budget review time, we may make submissions for additional money in any of the code areas based on justifiable needs. These needs may or may not be met depending on other priorities and the state of the economy. The actual allocation of funds at the school level is left to the discretion of the principal.

3. Community relationship building   The school is proud to call itself a community school. The school letterhead boasts 'School and community/ partners in education'. This has a number of implications, the first of which is legal. There exists between the City of Moose Jaw and the Board of Education an agreement for the joint use of facilities. An official community-use committee presides over the use of the school facility after school closing. The principal or a designate sits on this committee. Our committee has functioned as an informed parent-advisory committee, a parent-support network, as well as programme developer for the use of the school, and as a group that helps us to raise funds. I consider this group vital to our success.

4. Curriculum development   This involves monitoring the use of the curricula already in place. The principal needs to be in a position to reassure parents that curricula are being followed.

5. Discipline   School rules are kept to a minimum. They are carefully spelt out for parents in the handbook that is given out at an information night at the beginning of each year. Discipline matters that reach the principal are dealt with via an action plan, which is a mutual contract between the student and the school.

6. Facility inspection   For effective maintenance of school facilities, there needs to be a constant monitoring and communication to maintain positive staff and student relationships. A weekly walk-through with the caretaker is a quick way to clear up concerns either group may have.

7. Liaison with central office   As well as keeping relationships running smoothly within the school, ongoing communication must flourish with central-office (LEA) personnel. Encouraging staff to use the consulting services may involve setting up schedules or freeing a staff member from classroom duties so he or she can have time with the consultant.

8. Parental-concerns identification   Parental concerns are dealt with as efficiently and effectively as possible. It is important that the message reaching the community is that the school is approachable, caring and capable. New parents are telephoned within two weeks of enrollment to see how well their children are 'settling in' from the home's point of view, and whether there are any adjustment problems.

9. Priorities checking   The efficient and effective completion of these priorities is part of the administrative team's evaluation in June. Periodic monitoring keeps these on target.

10. Professional development   The principal is one member of a committee responsible for encouraging professional development at the school level. This group meets regularly to allot money for participation in conferences and it may initiate school-based in-service to meet the school's particular needs.

11. Professional duties   Professional duties include attendance at one principal's meeting per month, working on system-level committees or projects, attending conferences or seminars for updating skills and setting personal-improvement goals.

12. Public relations   Public relations include not only our communication with parents but also our involvement with the larger community that surrounds our school. In Saskatchewan, we estimate that approximately 70 per cent of the tax-payers who support our schools through their taxes have no children in attendance at our schools. To ensure their ongoing support for funding public education or to enhance the possibility of their positive response at times when there is a call for public money to fund building expansions, it is crucial that they value the school. We believe they will appreciate educational activities more if they see the school in action. We encourage community volunteers, hold open houses, tour senior-citizen centres, join in community projects and say 'thank you' often through advertisements, newsletters and school-appreciation programmes.

13. School-improvement monitoring   At present we are involved in two school-improvement initiatives. One is a well-defined, ongoing project that continuously generates opportunities for school improvement. The provincial cadre are able to offer up-to-date research and ideas as well as training in effective group processes by which to attain these directions. Local school boards may buy into the training or network with existing projects.

The second and probably most important initiative is the development of a core curriculum. These basic subjects are achieved through processes known as 'common essential learnings'. Over the next ten years all the curricula in the province will be redesigned to reflect basic knowledge and processes of common essential learnings. This is a monumental investment for both the Provincial Department of Education and the local school boards. School divisions are offered the opportunity to be a part of the curriculum development by supplying expertise in the area of curriculum design and also piloting the proposed curricula projects and recommending revisions.

14. Staff duties   All staff members, including administrators, need to assume responsibility for the many tasks that exist outside the main educational process. The principal serves as a role model in this area.

15. Supervision of staff   Supervision of staff is the latest duty Saskatchewan principals have assumed. In our system, principals are expected to conduct three, formal, classroom visits per teacher per year. These are full-scale formal visits with a preconference, the visit, a postconference and a written report. In addition, following the successful business-management technique, MBWA (management by walking around), I find that brief visits to all classrooms on a daily or a twice-weekly basis enable me to have a better intuitive grasp of the direction our educational tasks are taking. The whole concept of principal supervision still has some potential philosophical negatives to overcome in Saskatchewan. Two of these are as follows:

- Can a principal do formative and summative evaluation without jeopardizing one or both of these positions?
- Are principals trained sufficiently for these tasks?

I understand the reservations but feel comfortable with the results of my personal experiences.

Our system, after a number of consensus-establishing meetings by a cross-section of the various stakeholders, was able to develop four booklets that contain indicators of successful teachers, administrators, clerical aides and maintenance personnel. These are not a checklist but form an excellence basis for discussion.

ORGANIZATION AND MANAGEMENT OF LEARNING

Learning in Saskatchewan is standardized across the province by the nature of its curricula. For the elementary school there are no province-wide exams. A rather modified continuous-progress plan places all students in grade one by the age of 6 and ensures that students will progress systematically from grade one to twelve.

Periodically there is a great deal of concern that elementary schools do not do an effective job of teaching the basics. The basis for this criticism is a general concern by higher-learning institutions (universities and post-secondary colleges) that the general ability of their students to write and spell and to compute is lower than it used to be.

There is a good deal of truth to these concerns. What is not enunciated clearly is that, at all levels, classteachers are getting a greater span of abilities with which to work than ever before. The very bright students now have the advantage of world exposure because of television and increased travel opportunities. The severely handicapped who, three decades ago, had little chance for survival, may now be in the mainstream classroom for at least a part of the day. There is an expectation that all these students of such varied abilities will achieve, whether by a regular or a modified route, the equivalent of a grade-twelve standing in an integrated setting.

Within the Moose Jaw Public School Division, much planning is done on a system-wide basis to create programmes that meet the needs of special students. Schools assign students to these programmes on the basis of predetermined entrance criteria. If the programme is being offered in a school other than the student's home school, transportation is provided. The underlying philosophical base is to provide education for all students in the least-restrictive appropriate environment, with as much peer interaction as possible. In the midst of all this, the classteacher works diligently to transfer the common essential learnings into the existing curriculum, to adapt for the disadvantaged and to enrich the gifted.

It is important to note that, beneficial as these services are, they add significantly to the duties and responsibilities of the school administrator. Schedules must be carefully developed and closely monitored so that school activities do not conflict negatively with special services. It must also be ensured that services are appropriately and consistently provided. It also falls to the administrator to co-ordinate the team meetings whereby parents, resource personnel and teachers discuss the programme for the child and monitor the child's success on a regular basis.

RELATIONSHIPS

The network of relationships within the school setting is very complex. Teachers in Saskatchewan must now hold the equivalent of a four-year BEd degree before they can be considered for a teaching position. If they are graduates of a Saskatchewan University this means they have had a fairly extensive classroom-apprenticeship programme.

Once in the field, teachers are hired to the school division. Their individual assignment to a school is done in consultation with the school's principal. While principals cannot hire directly, they provide a clear picture of the type of person who will fill the void in their particular programme. The system welcomes the new teachers with a short orientation and an information package. It is then up to the school to see that teachers are conversant with current practices and policies. All teachers in Saskatchewan must be members of the Saskatchewan Teachers Federation. The objectives of this organization have virtually remained unchanged since the passing of its statutory recognition in 1935. Its basic function is to promote the cause of both education and teacher welfare.

Teachers must have two years with the division before they become members of the permanent staff and are entitled to the full privileges of job security. The principal, in conjunction with Central Office staff, is responsible for supervision and assessment of the performance of these teachers.

There is an expectation that teachers will share in both student extracurricular duties and professional staff duties. Generally, staff find it rewarding to become better acquainted with students of other grade levels and to network in an adult setting with staff from their own and other schools.

Staff receive three preparation periods per week (of 37 minutes each). Prior to 1987 elementary staff received no prep time, so this is a relatively new experience for us. Everyone in the school system receives the last period on Friday afternoon. Internal coverage will provide for the other two periods. Some additional staffing has made this easier to administer. However, there is still the occasional need for coverage by the principal or the librarian.

In accepting the position of principal of Sunningdale school, I had made it quite clear that my vision for this new school was that of a community school. Despite the fact that local politics are often based on uncertainty of purpose, there is a definite need to play a clearly defined role in the affairs of the larger community. I am pleased that our Board of Education provided an opportunity for latitude in decision-making such that I was able to create a unique model for providing educational services within our city.

I believe that community members, parents, business persons, senior citizens and pre-schoolers need to be involved in strong positive relationships with the school. In our case the task was uphill all the way. Citizens in this area had purchased residential property believing the school would be built in the centre of the sub-division. Now looking like the *Little House on the Prairie* (the title of a popular children's story by Laura Ingalls Wilder) the school was being constructed about a mile away from the sub-division on the other side of a creek. Surely, if children were not lost in the unprotected distance during a prairie winter blizzard, they would be drowned on a spring adventure!

As soon as stage one of the building programme (of portable classrooms) was complete, we began to establish traffic patterns towards the school with the offer of a programme of stories and activity for those children who would soon be kindergarten students. As principal-librarian in both my former school and initially the new school as well, I felt to be well in my element.

The school was to open in the portables for grades kindergarten–three, while the other eight classrooms and main core were constructed alongside. Anticipating a natural trauma in moving to a new school, we invited September's pupils and their families to attend a June pancake breakfast. Students met their new teachers and surveyed their new rooms. Children left filled with anticipation about the new school year.

Small though we might be, at least initially, we were a place for the community to meet. A Sunningdale Community Association was formed. Parents participated in the planning of the larger school and the programming of the smaller school. The city was successfully petitioned to increase our budget by $300,000 to enable us to erect an adult-size gym. This small political victory spurred the group on to further efforts with a newly founded confidence.

With the completion of the school, this relationship blossomed. A monthly, school newsletter keeps the community up to date on community affairs. The staff-room is labelled 'lounge' and parents are welcome at any time. Complimentary coffee is provided by the community association. This has some disadvantages but we find the positive public relations far outweigh the negatives.

Parents became willing volunteers around the school. They began a mammoth fund-raising campaign for playground equipment. They organized a pre-school programme to initiate students into 'their' school at an early age. Mothers held aerobics classes in free gym time.

A small collection of books from the public library enables members of the community to borrow books at school. During both day and evening, as space permits, the school is programmed for the community. Last year over 300 people participated in these opportunities such as crafts, aerobics, volley ball and cake-decorating. The Sunningdale Community Association works in conjunction with Wakamow Rotary Club to run bingo each month. The profits from this have financed road trips, purchased additional equipment and allowed us to reward groups, such as safety patrol. This extra income is greatly appreciated.

Initiatives have been taken to weld the various sectors of the community closer together. Last year we received a grant from the Saskatchewan Department of Health to organize an educational programme under the banner 'Everyone Wins'. Diversified Services, Sunningdale Community Church, Sunningdale School and the community association combined in an event that stressed nutrition, good physical well-being and a drug- and alcohol-free life-style. As well as uniting the community in a family-fun event, this project netted us approximately $1,000.

With a carefully worded newsletter that lavishly recorded our thanks, we began to move into the community for small, corporate, business donations. Once thanked in our newsletter, the corporate business remained on the mailing-list for the rest of the year. Sometimes even the hint of an upcoming event was enough to have offers of drinks for the students or prizes for the event from some of our previous sponsors.

Whenever there is public involvement there is tension. We have to be careful we do not become the advertising agency for any one business. We have to recognize that we are always on display. All in all it has been worth while. Our reputation for being open, caring, community minded and concerned has earned us a positive community image touted by estate agents and ordinary citizens.

The seven school trustees elected by the tax-payers of Moose Jaw have been consistently supportive of the school. Our trustees do not represent specific geographic areas but rather the city as a whole. Trustees are a policy-making group. They rely on the administrative and teaching staff to carry out their policy in a judicious manner and provide a supportive environment in which to function. The board had been sufficiently well informed on the progress of the school that, when we discovered a major need in the area of science supplies, they were willing to supplement the regular budget with additional funding.

The openness of the school leads to administrative time being required to work with the many volunteers who are in the building at any given time. We have developed a specific training programme for our volunteers to be offered at regular times throughout the year as well as a volunteer handbook.

Volunteers work in the office, classroom and library. They perform a variety of tasks under the direct supervision of the professional in charge of the area. Much of the work with the volunteers is adult education in disguise. A number of these people, once they are orientated to workplace routines and feel comfortable with their skills, go on to paying jobs either within the school system or elsewhere in the workforce.

To supplement our staff and to bring different insights into our environment, we also work with career-work students (grade-twelve students who may elect to work in the career of their choice for a term (part-time) as one of four electives). We accept Faculty of Education students from the University of Regina to receive practical classroom observation and training opportunities within our school. We work with the Department of Manpower and Immigration to assist people to develop basic work skills. We provide job opportunities for our system students who are in a life-skills programme.

Our staff has a number of talented people who serve on provincial subject councils and give workshops in their area of expertise. The Board of Education is generous in providing time for us to follow these pursuits and in allotting money for further professional development.

PERSONAL REFLECTIONS

The aspect of the job I value most is the opportunity to work closely with both adults and children – but especially with children. One can theorize brilliantly and plan minutely but the moment of truth lies with child contact. I have been privileged to capture some of those rare moments when a child recognizes the ability he or she possesses. I particularly remember one young boy who discovered mid-way down a flight of stairs that he could read the note to be taken home to his parents. The exhilaration of that moment made all of our efforts worth while.

I also value the opportunity to effect change. The principalship is not a static, predictable position. Within the routines are a thousand variations of situations. It is both possible and necessary to be a change agent, the bridge between theory and practice. This is an exceptional opportunity and one I deeply appreciate.

The aspect of the job I least enjoy is the paperwork. While I recognize the importance of adequate records, I delegate as much of this type of activity as I can. It would be very easy to become trapped in the office behind great mounds of memos and requests. I think it is important to attempt to keep one's desk clear and organized. Staff quickly become reluctant to discuss something with a person who is already deluged with work. The management theory for achieving this posture is excellent: my practice, however, still needs a great deal of work.

In the year of writing this contribution, my priorities for change included:

1. the development of a written set of expectations that can be shared with parents about our computer programming, kindergarten–8. As it stands now, not all classes have an equal opportunity to develop their skills; and

2. The development of an individualized programme for post-grade-eight students who wished to upgrade their academic skills before proceeding to high school. This may take the full academic year or just the first term of the high-school year.

Staff will undoubtedly have some additional group priorities that will be incorporated at our first staff meeting in September.

The job of principal is never finished. I do not think that anyone would want it otherwise. The challenge is never-ending. There are, however, some things though that would make the task more manageable.

We are in a period of tremendous change. Accelerating information, technological advancement and societal confusion are making an impact on staff and students alike. To survive this change, time is needed for reflection. Personal caring (known euphemistically as 'high touch') is needed within the school to offset high tech in the community. The school needs to be an island of stability in a world of rapid change.

Unless we can re-organize our structure dramatically, I believe we face confusion and frustration in the years ahead. It is interesting that, despite all the knowledge that has been amassed about learning and teaching styles and despite the fact that by the year 2000 information will be doubling rapidly, the basic school organization remains unchanged. When students arrive at the school in September, they are guaranteed 197 days of schooling with no more than ten days taken out for in-service training, reporting, etc. Students are placed in the classroom according to grade. There are approximately 23 students per class. While the desks are rarely in the straight rows of the past, much of the traditional structure does still remain.

Professional teachers need a great deal more time to prepare for new curriculum, to 'kid watch' and to reflect on the results, and to share their expertise with colleagues. Right now, highly trained professionals spend valuable instructional time doing tasks that could be done just as well by para-professionals (welfare and clerical assistants). Additional para-professional help could do such things as hunt for lost mittens, collect bus money and supervise incomplete homework – the list would be very long indeed.

This arrangement of additional para-professional staffing, coupled with variations in time of work, for example, a student day and a teacher day, a student year and a teacher year, could give education the impetus it needs to produce a more satisfactory product.

At present, education is one of the few businesses with a virtual monopoly. There is a very real danger that, while we sit complacently within our familiar structure, someone will devise a system of educating that better meets the needs of the child of the future. I want that person to be a caring educator rather than a shrewd business person.

If education is the foundation of our country, then the role of the principals can be likened to the work of good stone-masons. Principals are proud to be part of a very ancient craft. We recognize the importance of balancing new methods with tried and true practices. We accept the needs to apply extra effort in order to achieve success. Our ultimate reward is a fine finished project. Sunningdale School is just one of many Saskatchewan monuments to the future. I am pleased to be able to share its successes and its concerns with a wider public.

Commentary

Keerak stresses the need for a school retaining the confidence and support of a local community and of tax-payers (the majority of whom do not have children in the education system). She also expresses concern about being drawn, unwittingly, into unofficial public relations for commercial firms that sponsor school activities. Keerak is the only contributor to this collection of primary headteachers (unlike the secondary collection) to talk about 'management-by-walking-about' – maintaining a high level of visibility around the school.

She is not alone in describing the use of volunteer help, often parents, in the school, but what is unusual is the overt 'adult education' focus that often results in adult volunteers progressing to formal qualifications on the basis of new-found experience and confidence acquired in the school setting.

Interestingly, the Saskatchewan plan for common essential learnings bears some marked resemblances to the National Curriculum.

Like McDonnell (Chapter 1), Keerak expresses disquiet over external forces exerting too much influence on education only, in her case, the risk comes not from central government but from business interests.

7
Anne Waterhouse
Asmall County Primary School

Anne Waterhouse gained admission to Edge Hill College of Education with the minimum entry qualifications, where she undertook an infants/juniors course. She began teaching in 1968. Marriage and two children were the intended end of a not-very-promising career as an infants teacher in Skelmersdale New Town. A short period of supply and part-time teaching was brought to an end abruptly in 1976 when her contract was terminated in the first round of teaching-staff cuts. A request for voluntary redeployment back to Skelmersdale followed experience in a village school. A widening of teaching experiences, additional qualifications and increasing involvement in the National Union of Teachers preceded a period of fruitless deputy head-teacher interviews. Sympathetic counselling and encouragement led, against the odds, to her appointment as headteacher of Asmall County Primary School in January 1984. Involvement with NUT has continued. She is a member of the professional committees for Edge Hill College and Lancashire and Cumbria, as well as the National Curriculum Council Committee A.

THE SCHOOL

Asmall County Primary School is an open-plan building situated on the outskirts of the Lancashire market town of Ormskirk, in an area of surplus primary-school places. The immediate vicinity is not the sole catchment area. Since the school opened in 1972 and throughout the period of its three women headteachers, it has traditionally admitted children from a wide geographical area and has tended to appeal to parents who have been attracted by small classes and the emphasis on positive relationships.

In 1981 the LEA opened a unit for partially hearing children in the school. Over the years this has changed and developed. Up to twelve children with varying degrees of hearing loss can be included on the school roll. Some of the children are profoundly deaf and would have previously had to attend special schools. The children are supported in their mainstream classes and through withdrawal sessions with a qualified teacher of the deaf. Alongside the pattern of integration for the hearing-impaired children, the school has also established a positive policy of integration for children with other statemented special educational needs, including children with physical disabilities and moderate learning difficulties. This development has been supported by the LEA provision of additional teaching and non-teaching staff. The high staffing levels have enabled all the children in the school to benefit from working in smaller groups and have given the impetus to staff and governors to develop whole-school curriculum and planning policies.

Equal opportunities is taken seriously as a key element in the work of the school. The curriculum is structured to ensure that all the children have access to all the available learning experiences, according to the stated LEA entitlement policy. There are, however, difficulties in promoting multicultural education in a virtually all-white community. There is a danger that contrived topics intended to give wider experiences to the children can become trivialized and give narrow, stereotyped impressions instead. There are similar problems with inviting token visitors into the school. The staff and governors attempt to address these problems by encouraging all the children to appreciate individual differences and to develop tolerance to differing views and beliefs. Care is also taken with visual materials and resources to endeavour to ensure that stereotypes are not reinforced.

PERSONAL PHILOSOPHY OF EDUCATION

How can I describe my personal philosophy of education? This is one of those dreaded interview-type questions. In my mind it is quite simple. My job is all about children and helping them to make the best use of all possible opportunities to learn. I believe schools should not be about adults: they should be places for children. When I was studying for my Diploma in the Advanced Studies of Education (DASE) I discovered Denis Lawton's *An Introduction to Teaching and Learning*.[1] I was intrigued by his notion that, as children were deprived of their liberty by being compelled to be educated, they had the following 'rights':

1. to have the respect of their teachers;
2. to have a worthwhile curriculum;
3. not to have their time wasted unnecessarily;
4. to be treated fairly;
5. to be a member of a community or organisation with an adequate rule system;
6. to complain;
7. to choose some activities;
8. to participate in some aspects of decision-making.

(*Ibid.* p. 129)

These seemed so sensible that they are now firmly embedded into my own educational beliefs.

As I have already indicated, I believe that all children, regardless of gender, race or disability have an entitlement to similar educational experiences and expectations. It is the responsibility of adults and, in particular, teachers, to ensure that these experiences are real and meaningful. One of my anxieties about the Education Reform Act 1988 (ERA) is that children who are not easily able to experience 'normality' are going to be officially labelled. Through National Curriculum 'modifications' they will be excepted from activities their peers take for granted. I am proud to be described as 'child-centred' and feel disquiet about the elements of the current education reforms that seem to pay little regard to the children for whom the standards are supposedly to be improved.

While I believe that children learn most effectively through discovery methods, I do not agree that the teacher should just wait until a child is ready to use such strategies for learning. The role of the teacher goes beyond that of facilitator and should encompass that of being an enabler. The teacher is therefore crucial, not merely as the 'deliverer' (dreadful description) of teaching to a passive group but also as the planner and organizer of a learning environment. A school should not just be a place for teaching. A school must be seen as a place for learning, providing opportunities for learning for everyone – children and adults.

This takes me to the next element of my philosophy. Drama was one of my college subjects. I heard the actor, Jonathan Pryce, on the BBC radio programme, *Desert Island Discs*, describe the course, which he followed the year after me, as an easy option. This is not my recollection. All the sociology, psychology and philosophy elements of my teacher-training course seemed at that time to be complicated, irrelevant and boring. Drama offered a practical way of working 'with' children, not teaching 'at' them. Drama also seemed to provide non-threatening procedures to help children work through real-life and imaginary experiences. As well as an assessment strategy it could also be used as a practical method of enabling children to consolidate learning in other areas.

Much later in my teaching career, a two-year part-time course, leading to the award of an Associateship of the Drama Board in Education (ADB,Ed), enabled me to appreciate the value of psychology, philosophy and sociology in education I had so casually dismissed as a student. I also realized that, while I was having these experiences as a learner, I was developing my professional self-confidence and consequently was better able to undertake my work as a teacher.

The definition of aims and objectives has always been difficult for me to reconcile with life in a primary-school classroom. At the same time I recognize that careful and detailed planning is, and always has been, an absolute necessity for successful teaching and learning. Lawrence Stenhouse[2] provided me with two answers while adding to my developing educational philosophy. The notion of the teacher as a researcher couples teacher development with curriculum development. Education as a process rather than a set of objectives as described by Stenhouse resolved my own difficulties in coming to terms with 'aims and objectives'. Stenhouse is, of course, perfectly correct when he states that the weakness in the process model is that it is dependent upon the quality of the teacher and yet it is so true that 'this is also its greatest strength' (*ibid.* p. 96).

In attempting to manage a school, my philosophy of education rests upon the need to ensure that children are given the maximum opportunities to develop to their potential without fear of failure. Children should also be enabled to recognize their particular rights and contributions within, and to, the school as an organization. Children have a strong sense of fair play. Where they are encouraged to suggest and monitor appropriate codes of behaviour, at playtimes, for example, then these 'rules' are accepted and followed, generally without argument. A spate of minor weekend vandalism was partially solved by appointing some of the children who tended to misuse the premises as 'building officers'. They took their morning patrols and record book very seriously and the weekend problems virtually disappeared. Following complaints from some of the children about an unfair grading system for girls and boys in an athletics programme, they were encouraged to write to the national organizers who responded by setting the children a challenge to make properly researched suggestions. It is intended to pursue these investigations and comparisons during the next athletics season, using the appropriate National Curriculum programmes of study. Charities seeking the support of the school have to deal with the charities committee consisting of interested children from throughout the school, who make decisions about which charities to help and in what way. All such real responsibilities support the curriculum work of the school as well as the personal development of the children (and keep staff on our toes).

At the same time the role of the teachers and all other staff working in the school should be perceived within the context of a learning as well as a teaching environment. All members of staff should have an acknowledged responsibility to share in whole-school problem-solving and decision-making. It is important for everyone, staff and children, to develop confidence in their own abilities. No one should be afraid of trying things out. It is perfectly acceptable to have several attempts to achieve eventual success. Democratic decision-making does have drawbacks. It is very time-consuming but, in my experience, is generally more successful than decisions made without reference to the other people involved.

MANAGEMENT-STYLE ROLE MODELS

I suppose my style of headship is an amalgam from all the different head-teachers who have influenced my personal development over the years. My first contact with a headteacher was during my own primary-school years. To a child she seemed to be a huge, loud woman whose size trebled after I had been 'rulered' by her during school assembly one morning for telling lies. (Only, of course, I didn't, but they all say that, don't they?) In actual fact, when I went back to visit her shortly before she retired and after I had started teaching, she was a perfectly normal, reasonable person who ran a successful school. The moral in this tale is always to be sure before embarking on drastic actions, regardless of whom they concern, but particularly when children are involved.

When I started teaching I was lucky to be able to work for one of those charismatic headteachers who seemed to have the ability to get anyone to do anything. I still remember one very good piece of advice from the early period of my career. The head told me to stop worrying so much and that, provided I was properly organized, the children would learn in spite of me. At that time he appeared to be an inveterate 'fence-sitter', much to my frustration. It was only later that I appreciated his art of deciding not to make a decision. Experience consistently illustrates that, like him, when I take time to think things through my decisions are usually reasonable, but big decisions taken 'on the hoof' are invariably disastrous.

Another example of successful headship was an infant-school head, who ruled her school with a rod of iron. Everyone quaked when she appeared. It was the days when teachers had been released from 'doing' the dinner money and dinner duties. After much prompting from home I broached the subject and said that I was not going to collect and account for the money any more. 'We all do it here, dear', was the response . . . I carried on collecting it! I admired the power of her personality tremendously and still envy her apparent ability to make organization appear so easy. However, it seemed to me that to use fear as a management tool is inappropriate, particularly with young children.

The head of a village Church of England school provided my next example. The reception children in my class and I were new to the school at the same time. We all managed remarkably well, considering the circumstances. The trauma of that experience convinced me that new children *and* staff need support when beginning a new school. I could not at first understand why he had appointed me. It was he, however, who made me realize that perhaps I had the makings of a career teacher. I felt as if he was using me as a catalyst within the staff. For the first time I began to understand the powerful effects of different teaching styles. The school was judged to be successful within its community but I was very unhappy. In sticking to my 'child-centred' views I felt I was working against the long-term interests of the children. The experience made me realize the importance of a staff team. I also realized the need to use different staff strengths at different times for different purposes.

Subsequently I worked for the local secretary for the National Association of Headteachers (NAHT) at the time when I became the local secretary for the National Union of Teachers (NUT). As headteacher he created the ambience for the staff to experiment and to try out their own ideas. The school was open plan and his views did not always please the parents. He was very innovative and good for staff development. There seemed to be, however, little coherent planning, record-keeping or overall curriculum policy. There was little apparent consistency of approach. As children moved through the school they had to adjust to the different styles of successive teachers. I was promoted to a language co-ordinator scale-two post during my second term in the school. Provided we could justify what we wanted, and persuade our colleagues to follow our proposals, each co-ordinator was given valuable management experience in being able to initiate and develop our own curriculum areas. At the time, I felt concern that the head did not really know what we were doing, although with later experience I began to appreciate his actual levels of perception.

It was during this period that he encouraged me to work towards my DASE. I opted for a course on curriculum theory and practice. My studies supported my growing belief that there should be some sort of nationally agreed core curriculum. I felt that it was unreasonable for individual teachers to have to decide an appropriate curriculum for their pupils, plan it, find the resources and make all the assessment and evaluation decisions on their own. However, the DES publication on the curriculum[3] was far too utilitarian for my developing educational thinking. With hindsight I believe that this particular document was one of the first major pieces in a political jig-saw puzzle that was completed with ERA.

My involvement with NUT has given me valuable experience in dealing with a range of people and enabled me to keep up with, and often keep ahead of, national and local developments. As a newly appointed head-teacher, I was determined to follow the advice of my first head and never expect the staff to do anything I was not prepared to do myself. As time passes this is becoming harder to accomplish, particularly as classteachers become more familiar with the day-to-day operation of the National Curriculum structures and I still struggle with the paperwork. I keenly remember my own previous annoyance at never really understanding how my work related to the school as a whole and at never having enough information about what was going on. As a new headteacher I was also determined to put into practice all the strategies I had learnt through experience as well as selecting from the variety of examples demonstrated by my role models.

SCHOOL ORGANIZATION

When Neville Bennett[4] was undertaking his research into formal and informal primary education in the late 1970s, the school was used in a BBC *Horizon* documentary programme as the example of an informal organization. The programme was supporting Bennett's 'findings' and the school was used to represent the 'failings' of informal schools. Asmall School, unfairly in my view, was not represented in a positive light. When I became the head the staff were still feeling vulnerable and lacking in professional confidence. I invited a range of people into school to help us examine our organization and curriculum. From their comments and our own conclusions we were reassured about our general aims and philosophy but accepted the need to sharpen up our practice.

After six years at Asmall School I am concerned that the implementation of ERA could well affect its viability. This is causing me to reconsider my management strategies and style of leadership. I do not consider that the leader has always to be 'up front'; it is often more effective to lead from behind. There are tensions between this approach and school marketing creating the need for a more overt style of public relations. At the same time, whole-school management and decision-making should mean just that. If members of a team do not feel that consultation is real, then I believe that the exercise is meaningless. Staff can become even more cynical when no consultation takes place. This has caused me difficulties over the years but I have always tried to be honest in my dealings with staff, children, parents and everyone else. Obviously as the headteacher I am paid to make decisions and accept responsibility at the end of the line but, for the school to work as a coherent whole, everyone must be involved and I must be prepared to give my reasons for my eventual decisions.

This whole-school commitment places very high demands on everyone involved. The staff at Asmall are tremendous. They are prepared to have a go at anything they consider worth while. Everyone, teaching and non-teaching staff alike, is interested in the children. All the staff know all the children, and all the children know all the staff. The children are expected to treat all adults working in the school with the same respect. Generally speaking there are few problems with behaviour. The staff need no encouragement to respect the children.

The school has about 135 children on roll who, until now, have been organized into five classes. I have worked in both traditionally organized and vertically grouped classes. Experience has led me to share John Barrett's contention that 'there is a considerable benefit in vertical grouping for both the child and the teacher'.[5] I also share Barrett's view that the success of such grouping depends on the commitment of 'reflective' teachers, to the agreed aims and principles of the school. Such teachers also believe that schools are for 'the development of the individual', and that the way children are organized and grouped affects their development (*ibid.* p. 26). Primary-age children need stability and the space and time to develop at their own pace. Vertical grouping gives them this opportunity. It also gives flexibility to keep siblings or unsuitable friends apart if necessary. Room for manoeuvre, where there are personality clashes, is also important, and difficult to achieve in a small school. The children and I are lucky that the staff at Asmall support these principles. The staff generally share my view that the National Curriculum structure, promoting and enabling children to work at their own appropriate levels, is also a strong argument in favour of vertical grouping.

The change in parental perceptions about mixed-age classes has been interesting. A few years ago some parents were concerned that such classes might hold back their children. Over the years some children have been removed to larger, neighbouring schools with more traditional class organization but, conversely, others have moved to us because of our smaller classes and the way in which we try to view all children as individuals. Generally speaking, our children more than hold their own through secondary education. We are often told how positively our children approach new experiences and are able to undertake independent learning.

The pattern of organization cannot remain fixed for each year as it depends on the numbers of children leaving and being admitted. In the light of organizational changes resulting from the National Curriculum, we have been considering a move away from the traditional primary-school class-teaching model. The teacher who takes the register, with responsibility for the pastoral care of each child, does not necessarily have to teach that child all day for every curriculum area. I visited a school in another LEA where such a pattern of organization existed and was impressed by the possibilities. Such organization would have to be tightly structured and I can see that there could well be conflicts of interest as we try also to retain the flexibility that is a feature of good primary practice. The removal of the barriers presented by class teaching would enable the staff to make more efficient use of the children's time. It would also enable more of the successful cross-age-group teaching that has been evolving recently to take place. Such a drastic change depends on staff consistency. Unfortunately, in practice these plans had to be modified. My lengthy absence from school, due to illness, necessitated the deputy having to leave his class while assuming the responsibilities of acting headteacher. Difficulties in finding supply-teacher cover meant the children having to work with several different teachers who were all unfamiliar with the school. The constraints caused by staffing problems have led to the postponement, for the time being, of radical changes in organization.

Apart from the organizational problems that can beset any school, the nature of the open-plan building enables the staff to work co-operatively but, at the same time, provides constraints. There is very little central storage space and no permanent storage or display surfaces in the teaching areas. This makes the organization of physical resources very difficult and limits the amount of interactive three-dimensional display work that can be undertaken. It also means the place always looks untidy. The storage of science materials, art and craft resources and PE equipment is the most difficult. One of the benefits of schools accepting more responsibility for the buildings is that, for the first time, we are in a position to initiate our own improvements. Capital building repairs are providing the opportunity for the staff to make recommendations for better storage and display areas. This should improve the organization and use of resources and teaching areas.

ORGANIZATION AND MANAGEMENT OF LEARNING

My involvement with the union has meant that I have been able to keep abreast of developments in the wider educational world. It is all too easy for the teaching staff in a school to become very inward looking and to lose sight of the wider context in which they are supposed to operate. Right from the beginning of my headship I have attempted to keep the school and the staff in touch with the outside world. Prior to ERA we tried to respond to those developments we judged would be of benefit to our work. Even where there was not the time to send official responses, for example, to DES discussion papers, we read them and identified areas where we needed to improve our practice. We also had early warning about LEA initiatives, because of my union involvement, and were able to consider the implications of these in our own time, without the pressure of mandatory changes. This experience has sustained us for the unprecedented introduction of the National Curriculum.

It is something of an understatement to say that we could have done without the National Curriculum just at the moment. As a staff we decided that, although initially it was only compulsory for one year group, we would in practice introduce the National Curriculum throughout the school as information about each subject area became available. This would enable us to work into the subjects at our own pace. We decided against spending hours of staff-meeting time trying to understand it all, instead – on the basis of learning through experience – we have actually tried to work through the core subjects of maths, English, science and now technology.

During the summer term 1989 we held a parents' evening to explain our understanding of what were the implications for the school. An outside speaker from a university agreed to come to describe the national context, while the staff and I tried to relate it to what we were doing at school. The meeting was successful and parents were reassured that we seemed to know what we were doing (so were we!). Everyone was also impressed by the fact that a renowned academic was willing to come to talk to our small school community.

However, a bad dose of the National Curriculum heebie-jeebies beset the school during the autumn term 1989. There was absolutely no alternative but to work through the wretched ring-folders of curriculum materials that seemed to arrive by parcel post on an almost daily basis. It has been soul destroying trying to become familiar with the seemingly endless attainment targets and statements of attainment. Although we agree among ourselves that the programmes of study and the processes of learning are important elements, our awareness of the requirements to report to parents and others in a yet-to-be-prescribed form on the basis of statutory National Curriculum structures has caused additional unpleasant tensions for us.

A very bland matrix checksheet was introduced for each child to provide a see-at-a-glance-what-level record. At the end of the first term I collected examples of these from each year group and plotted them on a master sheet to see if there was progression throughout the school. With relief I was able to confirm the progression, although subsequent exercises have raised further questions about the need for moderation and agreed definitions between the teaching staff. We have resisted the temptations to try to evolve, or use, more sophisticated checklists on the basis that matters are already complicated enough. Anyway, I believe that we owe each child more than mere ticks on a 'tick-list'.

It has been a source of cynical delight to note the DES back-pedalling on the complex arrangements for assessment. Reported comments suggest that the former Prime Minister was not expecting the National Curriculum to be so detailed. The terms of reference for the subject working parties for art, music and physical education certainly require less detail for the final reports. Debates about the history and geography reports also indicate a growing political awareness of the pressures on time. However, government circulars about the use of time indicate that the civil servants at the DES still have much to learn about what really happens in our schools.

Although we feel that the National Curriculum, as it stands, is too detailed, as a staff our experience so far indicates that the structures help us to sharpen up our practice. I am not sure that the present emphasis on levels means that we are better able to ensure that all children are able to experience appropriate learning opportunities. We believe that assessment by teachers could be improved and the School Examinations and Assessment Council (SEAC) packs have helped us to define and improve our own practice. The SEAC materials, however, could have been much more 'user friendly'. Helpful suggestions and guidelines are buried too deep within them. We are reserving judgement about the standard assessment tasks (SATs).

The financial implications of ERA are causing problems, as will the publication of the results of testing, even though this will no longer be compulsory for 7-year-old children. On paper Asmall School is relatively expensive to run. In practice we are very cost effective. Without us, some of our children would have to attend 'out-county' special schools with their accompanying high fees. Testing and the publication of results is a dilemma on two counts. Children cannot all be expected to achieve at 'normal' levels. Published test results, together with a financial league-table, will misrepresent the achievements of children and of schools.

In terms of organization and management for learning, I am extremely fortunate to be working with colleagues who are thoroughly professional in all they do. The best interests of the children are at the centre of the organization. As experience develops, the staff are becoming more and more sensitive to the needs of all children and are becoming more proficient in meeting varied needs. The staff are justifiably proud of their work in developing strategies for integrating children with special educational needs into the school. The philosophy of the school is clear in that all children have an entitlement to the same educational opportunities. The staff are equally clear in their collective view that it is their responsibility to enable children to benefit from the learning experiences available within the school. The inclusion of the hearing-impaired children within the school has provided the stimulus for coherent curriculum planning and organization. The introduction and implementation of the National Curriculum has been both supportive and counter-productive in terms of our own school-based curriculum development.

RELATIONSHIPS

Successful teaching and learning is dependent upon good relationships between all the participants. This makes staff selection of vital importance to the future success of the school. I have very strong views about the way in which prospective staff for schools are interviewed. I believe that the ownership of the interview should lie with the person being interviewed. A successful appointment is just as important for the individual candidate as it is for the organization, if not more so. Consequently, all the teaching and non-teaching staff who are interviewed for positions at Asmall School experience a relatively hard selection process. Each member of the team has an important role to play in the work of the school. If a wrong appointment is made, whether for caretaker, cook or headteacher, then this has repercussions on the team as a whole. At Asmall we try to ensure that candidates are fully aware of what is expected and give people the opportunity to withdraw if they wish. It is also important for the existing members of the team to feel that they have a role to play in the selection procedure for new colleagues, although this is obviously limited. There is little logic in appointing the ideal candidate on paper if it seems that there is going to be a clash of personalities. However, it is also important for existing staff to appreciate that different strengths are also needed at different times.

In the time I have been headteacher at Asmall, I have worked with three deputies. Each of them has been successful but in different ways. My first deputy was very child-oriented. She had been with the school since it opened and this was an internal promotion. She helped and supported me at the beginning of my headship and I greatly appreciated her professionalism. We were delighted for her when she obtained her well-deserved headship. Her promotion enabled me to make my first staff appointment as we sought her replacement. The staff of the school are a very stable crew but at that time needed someone who could help them to look outwards and to feel more confidence in themselves and the work of the school. The deputy also needed to be someone who could easily establish relationships with parents and governors. I had made the mistake of trying to do too much too soon, without first clearing the way, and consequently had upset the Friends of the School and the governors. The person appointed was successful in his deputy headship. He could charm the birds from the trees and is continuing to do so in his own school. His successful professional development was a credit to the whole-staff teamwork of the school and to his own commitment to primary-aged children.

The appointment of my third deputy, who began work with us in September 1989, has seen the beginning of a new phase in the development of the school. Previously we felt we were a successful 'child-orientated' establishment. The deputy is now helping the school to move into a phase of rapidly developing professional confidence in our curriculum structure, without losing sight of the needs of the children. At the same time he is building stronger relationships than ever with staff and parents. Asmall School whole-staff commitment enables positive relationships to be established and newcomers into the team seem to be infected with these qualities very rapidly. Trust and professional self-confidence in one's own abilities and those of colleagues are key elements in a successful pattern of relationships. The new deputy had to prove his competence with staff, children, parents and governors very quickly because of my unavoidable absence. He is likely to follow his successful predecessors sooner than I would wish in the staff-development cycle of the school.

Staff development is a very important element within my role as headteacher. I find it personally difficult to implement this responsibility. As a staff we are developing strategies for identifying and agreeing strengths and weaknesses. During the summer term of 1990 we began to use a format similar to the suggestions contained in the National Steering Group Report on Appraisal.[6] These procedures, however, make me feel very anxious. I do not feel confident or competent to sit in judgement on my colleagues. I feel that I am raising awareness and expectations in staff on which I may not be able to deliver. The staff, to their credit, have responded in their usual positive and supportive manner, and their responses have helped me to see more value in the procedures than I originally envisaged. Now I think that Evans and Tomlinson[7] were correct in their assertion that 'classroom teachers will be able, in a way that has not been possible in the past, to set an agenda for change of their own'. Although I do not like the part I have to play in the process, I think appraisal is going to be a positive element for staff-development policies in the future. Appraisal for headteachers has to be part of the process but I feel a great sense of personal unease over the means by which this may be undertaken. It is important for all appraisers to appreciate and understand the context in which the appraisal is being undertaken. External appraisal of headteachers is likely to make this very difficult to achieve.

In the wider context of developing external relationships, open enrolment is a feature of ERA that causes me great unease. Over the past five years there has been a growing positive trend for the staffs of schools to develop strategies for working together. The advent of the five non-teaching days, the transformation of identifying and providing in-service education and training (INSET) into school and 'cluster' activities across neighbouring schools, have enabled teachers from these different schools to benefit from a wider range of experiences. A considerable amount of liaison has been developing between primary and secondary schools. Open enrolment may well put all these developments at risk. Colleagues from nearby schools are less likely to share ideas and experiences when they are in competition for children in order to maintain the financial viability of individual schools. Open enrolment is also going to make the notion of National Curriculum moderation very difficult. It is not easy for teachers in different schools to have sufficient professional confidence in themselves, and trust within working relationships, to feel happy about revealing their weaknesses within neighbouring schools. To have to work in this way with colleagues who are in direct competition for 'customers' is going to cause many anxieties in the future.

The changing role of LEA advisers, as a result of the development of more inspectorial responsibility, is also going to change one very important set of relationships for teachers and headteachers, in Lancashire at least. I have always valued the advice given by the team of advisers in the county. I have not always agreed with, nor have I always liked, what has been said. As a new head, particularly, there were times when I needed someone to whom I could talk in confidence. I am very concerned that there is no longer going to be the opportunity to seek this sort of advice. Moreover, I am not sure that, even if they were to have the time, 'inspectors' are the appropriate people to whom problems should be revealed. One sad consequence of the pressures of the recent education Acts has been the number of our county advisers, as well as teacher colleagues, who have worked themselves into serious ill-health. To see respected colleagues leaving the education service under these circumstances suggests to me that something is wrong somewhere.

Another consequence of the 1986 and 1988 Education Acts has been the changing relationships with school governors. During my period of headship at Asmall School the governors have been considered as members of the school community. I have always sought to involve them and have never seen it as my role merely to inform them of my actions. I have tried to consult on all pertinent issues. Governors who have previously been closely involved are finding it harder to give the greatly increased time commitment required. I am aware that my expectations of lay people, not generally connected with education, are unreasonable in comparison with many other heads. I believe that individuals who seek to become school governors should be aware of the increased time commitment needed to fulfil their greatly increased statutory responsibilities.

This makes me sound as if I am not appreciative of the individual members of my governing body. I have been fortunate over the years with the governors willing to serve Asmall School. However, I feel concern over the pressures resulting from the increased responsibilities of governors from both the perspective of the school and for the people involved. As far as I am concerned, schools are places for children to experience effective teaching and learning. In my opinion schools can never be run as cost-effective businesses with the children seen mainly as the resources, and the parents as the customers. I am, perhaps, too vehement in my declaration that I am not interested in finance and only concerned with children, but I really believe that we – that is, headteachers and governors – should not be making a bad system work at the cost of the children's education. Local management of schools does have its advantages but, in my view, the notion of age-weighted pupil-driven formula funding is wrong.

Surprisingly, I find relationships with the unions difficult. As a member of a teaching union rather than a headteachers' association I feel able to anticipate the response of teachers to certain views. I also feel frustrated by the growing divisions between the unions. It appears to me to be increasingly difficult for teachers and heads to appreciate the nature of their different roles. Heads and teachers obviously do not have the same long- and short-term goals, but I believe that our schools would be very different places today if headteachers had not established their own associations, protecting one set of professional interests. The growth of separate unions has resulted in a rapid fragmentation of the profession. United we could have stood together, divided we have reached rock bottom. Perhaps the establishment of a general teaching council, with all branches of the education service equally and properly represented, will be the hope for the long-term future.

PERSONAL REFLECTIONS

Looking back, I do not really know what I expected in my brave new world starting in January 1984. It is fitting that I should be asked to reflect upon my headship during the same weeks as my first intake of reception children transfer into secondary education. I think perhaps I could have chosen a better time to become a headteacher. On the other hand, as I look round our school and consider what we have achieved, I wonder whether we could have done as much that is undoubtedly of educational value for the children without outside 'interference'. I feel a tremendous sense of pride as I look at the children moving onto the next phase of their formal education, and consider how they have developed over the years. I look at the staff, whom I have already described as the most consistently professional group of people any headteacher could hope to work with, and feel pride in their achievements. Nothing can quite compare with the feeling I experience when I walk round the building and see the school at work – on a good day of course! In contrast, no one prepared me for the work-related stress. I was not expecting to experience anxiety attacks when the school-gate 'mafia' is in full spate. I was not expecting to have to act in the role of counsellor for a wide range of personal and social problems. I often feel a 'jack of all trades but master of none'! I do not feel sufficiently competent to fulfil the business management role into which I have now been thrust. I have no training in accountancy. The children in my school are not pieces of machinery or financial units and, as a professional educator, I resent having to be part of a system that treats them as such.

As for the future, when I can overcome my cynicism, I have to admit these are exciting times. I am proud to have been invited to contribute, albeit in a minor way, to the national development of the National Curriculum Council. Once the subject curriculum components are all out in the open there is undoubtedly going to have to be a considerable amount of modification. I have been greatly reassured to discover that the National Curriculum ring-files and their contents are not tablets of stone. There is a considerable amount of work and commendable effort being undertaken by teachers and organizations such as the National Curriculum Council to develop a workable entitlement curriculum with an emphasis on good practice. As I noted earlier, I reserve my judgement about the assessment procedures. No teacher can teach successfully without assessing his or her own and the pupils' work, but the present proposals seem to be more about accountability than evaluation.

The greatest problems facing headteachers in the 1990s seem to me to revolve around the concept of formula funding. I am not interested in filling my school with age-weighted pupil units. I am determined to ensure that the best possible learning opportunities are available for all the children in my care. I am not sure that these two objectives are compatible. As a primary-school head I have amazed myself with what I have been able to achieve. I continue to feel humbled by the ever-growing realization that, despite all the education Acts in the world, I can only operate successfully with the consent and support of my colleagues, the trust of the parents and the mutual respect of the children. For all its failings and the misunderstandings, many of which were generated by misreporting, the Plowden Report was right to remind us, back in 1967, that 'at the heart of the process lies the child'.[8]

Commentary

Waterhouse's notion of a child-centred school, with the head an 'enabler' rather than 'deliverer', extends to the pupils' own contribution to policy and practice. The composition of Waterhouse's school, in a virtually all-white community, is very different from Smith's (Chapter 2). None the less, Waterhouse is concerned to promote multicultural education as part of the equal-opportunities entitlement.

Like Morton (Chapter 3), Waterhouse acknowledges that the early underpinnings of her training needed a practical catalyst – in her case, drama – to enable them to make sense. She is aware of the benefits of sometimes 'leading from behind', although she recognizes the tension between this approach and the new aggressive style of headship that is advocated as essential to the marketing of the school.

McDonnell (Chapter 1) considered, and rejected, a system of vertical grouping but it is a system favoured by Waterhouse and, moreover, one she deems entirely suitable to the structure of the National Curriculum. Going further, she raises interesting issues about the value of moving away from the traditional primary-school class-teaching model.

Waterhouse notes how her own union involvement has enabled her and, through her, her staff, to keep abreast of educational developments. Even as a head with long involvement in union activity, she has, at times, found the relationships with the unions over issues in her school difficult.

Like McDonnell, Waterhouse stresses the importance of the deputy's role, not least as a proving ground for aspiring headteachers. Somewhat surprisingly, she finds the head's role in staff appraisal anxiety-provoking. As yet – except for those areas involved with the pilot schemes – heads have not had to manage the appraisal process.

The issue of open enrolment and the possible negative consequences of competitive marketing and over-rivalrous heads is raised by her. She expresses fears about the potentially damaging effects of this on the other schools in her local 'clusters'.

REFERENCES

1. Lawton, D. (1981) *An Introduction to Teaching and Learning*, Hodder & Stoughton, Sevenoaks, p. 129.
2. Stenhouse, L. (1975) *An Introduction to Curriculum Research and Development*, Heinemann, London, pp. 142–65.
3. DES (1981) *The School Curriculum*, HMSO, London.
4. Bennett, N. (ed.) (1976) *Teaching Styles and Pupil Progress*, Open Books, London.
5. Barrett, J. (1988) Celebrating the vertically grouped class, in I. Craig (ed.) *Managing the Primary Classroom*, Longman, Harlow, pp. 25, 26.
6. DES (1989) *School Teacher Appraisal: A National Framework*, HMSO, London.
7. Evans, A. and Tomlinson, J. (eds.) (1989) *Teacher Appraisal: A National Approach*, Jessica Kingsley, London, p. 27.
8. Central Advisory Council for Education (CACE) (1967) *Children and their Primary Schools* (The Plowden Report), HMSO, London.

8
Peter Mortimore
Jo Mortimore
Issues in Primary Headship

The previous seven chapters have each presented the views of a head-teacher. These headteachers – as readers will have noted – are very different because of their age, background, gender or culture or because of their career experiences and the constraints of their current schools. They see their roles in slightly different ways. Nevertheless, they also share a number of views and attitudes towards the importance of schooling and pupils' learning and have made similar journeys, albeit from different starting-points and using various routes.

The seven heads have been guided, to a greater or lesser extent, by what they hold to be their philosophies shaped over many years and by a number of influences. Waterhouse acknowledges her debt to her experiences – not always positive – with previous headteachers, when she was a pupil at primary school and, later, a fledgling probationer and then an aspiring career teacher. For Keerak, living and working on the edge of the Canadian prairie, an in-service course by the American educator, Madeline Hunter, provided the charismatic spur to a whole new approach. The trauma and fatigue of Morton's first teaching post (with a class he was told was only there 'to be amused' and the bus window a welcome pillow on the journey home) reshaped his former theoretical perspective into a firm and enduring belief in the importance of teachers having high expectations of pupils who, in turn, have high expectations of themselves. Not surprisingly, people and relationships (sometimes pupils, sometimes the community of pupils, parents and staff) often have a place in the philosophy. Thus, for McDonnell 'schools are about people', whilst Morton considers that 'relationships are at the heart of learning'. For Waterhouse, 'schools are about children' and for Jones, 'children pass through primary school just once . . . we must ensure that this passage is a successful one'.

The importance of having a personal philosophy cannot be overstated. As so many of our contributors have reported, schools are currently being subjected to orchestrated changes. Some contributors welcome (at least some aspects of) the changes; others are more wary. At such times a personal philosophy, centred on the primacy of pupil-learning, provides a raft of support. Yet personal philosophies cannot be taught. No amount of instruction will lead automatically to their creation in any individual. As our contributors have so clearly identified, their genesis lies in personal history, reading, experience and, perhaps most of all, personal example. The power of modelling in teaching is unsurpassed. And each of these heads, in turn, is now a model for the next generation.

ORGANIZATION AND MANAGEMENT

Most of the contributors describe the challenges encountered when they first took up their headship post and the efforts and strategies involved in creating organizational structures within the school that allowed it to develop along the lines they believe to be important. This was easier in some cases than in others. In Keerak's school, for instance, there are clearly defined provincial duties that provide a framework. McDonnell faced a daunting task in seeking to mould a school community from a hetero-geneous group of twenty teachers from six different schools, teaching 470 pupils, on a split site!

Introducing and managing change is acknowledged by the contributors to be a slow and difficult process, yet probably a necessary one in order for schools to be living, vibrant institutions. As Morton says, 'there is rarely change without pain!' This pain has been illustrated in a number of chapters. There are examples of old-established staff enjoying 'curriculum autonomy' (Morton) and initially resisting change and of the various innovations that helped move things forward. These include staff task groups (McDonnell), whole-school projects and whole-school planning (Smith) and school self-evaluation (Wilcock); new in-class groupings (Morton) facilitated (in Jones's case) by her new furniture; and vertical grouping (Waterhouse). The latter three all comment how, in their view, the use of space and the ways in which children are grouped within it influences the development of learning. Other authors also comment on the influence of the environment on learning – either the prairie landscape in which the school is located (Keerak) or the more immediate open-plan surroundings in which learning is organized (McDonnell).

The importance of creating a management *team* and fostering a sense of endeavour and responsibility is also stressed by most contributors. Achieving this was not always an easy task, particularly for those heads whose new appointments coincided with national teacher action in the late 1980s. Morton, for example, writes movingly that his first two years in his current headship were 'the worst two years of my life'. Moreover, however democratic a head wishes, or is expected to be, he or she carries the final responsibility for what goes on in the school and must, at times, be prepared to make demands or decisions that will be unpopular with at least some staff or parents for some of the time. Thus Morton, keen to organize within-class grouping, found that 'no amount of hinting or suggestion brought about any change. In the end I had to ask that the new arrangements take effect by the following Monday'. Waterhouse, though striving to involve others in decision-making, recognizes that 'obviously as the headteacher I am paid to take decisions and accept responsibility at the end of the line . . . and I must be prepared to give reasons for my eventual decisions'.

The views of the seven heads on decision-making illustrate both the power and the limitations of headship. Interestingly, they mirror the findings of research on effective schools that has shown that heads are conscious of the *critical* decisions to be taken and about how to handle issues affecting the school. The research suggests that being too autocratic or too democratic has its problems. The skilful head has to decide on which occasions the decision has to be his or hers (even though – as Waterhouse has reminded us – he or she will have to account for it at a later stage) and on which occasions only a collective decision will enable ownerships of the matter to be taken by the staff. Possessing good judgement in this matter is an enormous advantage to a headteacher.

What is very clear from the chapters is that primary headteachers are having to spend much more time on management. This point is echoed by the senior chief HMI in his 1991 annual report.[1] He comments that his colleagues have detected signs that management and administrative duties are beginning 'to take their toll' (para 48, p. 8) on the curricular leadership of the heads of primary schools.

Of course, future generations of heads will come to expect a high proportion of management within the role of headship and, it is hoped, will be prepared to exercise it. It is this current generation of pre- and immediately post-ERA schools who face the challenge of new management tasks and

feel that their past has left them unprepared. Several contributors comment on the importance of providing their deputies with the opportunity to
develop management expertise. Some take pride in the subsequent promotion that is the almost inevitable consequence.

EDUCATION REFORM ACT 1988

Apart from Keerak in Saskatchewan, all the heads have been considerably
exercised over the introduction of the most far-reaching piece of educational legislation since 1944, the Education Reform Act 1988. The ramifica-
tions of the Act, particularly for the curriculum and school finances, are
addressed by all the British contributors. (Interestingly, Keerak describes
similar curriculum reforms now taking place that will result in a core curriculum of 'common essential learnings'.) Reactions to the National Curriculum and its associated assessment are mixed. Jones expresses the most
negative views that the guidelines carry 'paradoxical messages' expressing
'irreconcilable demands for both the structured and a cross-curricular approach'. The standard assessment tasks (SATs) – 'dreaded and feared' –
for which Jones's school was a pilot yielded, she claims, no more new
information about the pupils. No contributors welcomed the 'plethora of
documents' (McDonnell) – 'the wretched ring-folders' (Waterhouse) – that
threatened to overwhelm them and their hard-pressed staff. Some (heads
or their staff) expressed resentment at the 'haste and hassle' (Wilcock) and
reported teachers' pleas (to McDonnell) to 'give us a break, just for a
couple of weeks'. Overall, however, the National Curriculum structure is
welcomed for the way in which it highlights the need for 'a careful programme of school-focused curriculum change' (Smith) and enables children 'to work at their own appropriate levels' (Waterhouse). For Morton,
whose vision of education focuses on pupils' future contributions to
society, advantages lie in the support he sees in the National Curriculum
for personal, social and moral education. Wilcock considers that, in implementing the National Curriculum programmes of study, 'staff and pupils
are benefiting from more co-operative and mixed-ability teaching using a
cross-curricular approach'.

   This ambivalence (welcoming the principle of a National Curriculum and
grasping at its advantages, while regretting its prescriptive nature and fearing its consequences) is not peculiar to these headteachers. On this topic,
they surely speak for the profession.

   Since most of these heads completed their chapters, however, the situation has become more complex, with a third Secretary of State to hold

office since the Act came into being exploring his own powers and seeking to impose his own views on what the National Curriculum should be like. Such a situation breeds cynicism and may de-motivate the very people (i.e. headteachers) who have to translate the idea of the National Curriculum into reality for the pupils.

LOCAL MANAGEMENT OF SCHOOLS (LMS)

A number of contributors have experienced as pilot schools the financial delegation resulting from the LMS initiative. On the whole, they are positive about the increased autonomy and flexibility it provides – despite the headaches of reading gas and electricity meters and apportioning costs accordingly. The additional workload attendant upon LMS is not welcomed: the pressures of time management are commented upon by most. But the (in some cases) extra resources and the greater freedom in allocating them have resulted in the purchase of increased administrative support to help heads cope with the additional and changing financial and administrative demands now being placed on them. Indeed, Wilcock looks forwards to the time when she can appoint a bursar. Both Wilcock and Morton, however, also express disquiet at the potentially damaging effects on relationships with colleagues in neighbouring schools of the post-ERA 'marketing approach' to the competition for filling places through open enrolment.

These views illustrate the dilemma many heads currently have to face. How do they reconcile their duty to do the best for their own school – including filling all available places and, if necessary, buying in expertise in marketing in order to do so – with their loyalty to professional colleagues and their concern with the state of primary education in their area as a whole? There are, of course, no simple answers to such problems. The introduction of a 'market' economy to educational provision was not planned in order to make life easier for headteachers; far from it. The rationale of a market is that competition will force the providers (in this case the headteachers and governors) to offer the best value to the consumers (parents and pupils). On the other hand, heads in an area have to live alongside each other and competition deemed to be 'unfair' will be condemned by their peer group. Deciding whether marketing techniques are fair or unfair, in terms of competition with neighbouring schools, is likely to be tricky and to be outside the experience of most current heads. But it is the type of issue that will have to exercise their minds in the future.

GOVERNORS

Under both the 1986 Act and the Education Reform Act 1988, school governors have increased powers and responsibilities, the exercise of which called for a rethinking of relationships between a headteacher and his or her governing body. No longer can it be, in Morton's words, 'no better than that of a vicar hosting his own tea party'! Instead, an 'honest and open relationship has to be established through a process of team-building' (McDonnell) and parameter-exploring.

The theory underpinning the use of governing bodies is excellent – altruistic members of the community (whether parents, teachers or those just interested in schools), without any personal axes to grind, acting as a steering group for the headteacher and, collectively, taking on legal responsibilities for the functioning of the school. Unfortunately, in some cases, the practice fails to live up to the theory. Historically, governors (or managers, as primary-school governors used to be called) lacked power (as our contributors have noted) but they had responsibilities. However, as the excellent Auld report on the William Tyndale affair made clear, this did not free the LEA of its ultimate responsibility for the well-being of the school. Today, with a reduction in the power of LEAs brought about by the 1988 Act, governing bodies have far more power than was once the case. It is also clear from research that many governing bodies are not trained for or ready to shoulder such responsibility. Nor are some heads ready to accord governing bodies their full powers, as letters to the 'guru' of governing bodies (Joan Sallis) published in her *Times Educational Supplement* column make clear.

The contributors to this volume have been living through the transition from the old order to the new: hence their natural trepidation in not knowing whether to welcome, or regret, the changes. Those who have experienced supportive governing bodies that, nevertheless, demand accountability from the school, are likely to be positive. Any head (and this is not the sort of information that any of the contributors is likely to include) who has experienced the problem of a governor with a particular axe to grind and the subsequent disruptive effect on a school is likely to be less enthusiastic about the new powers.

PARENTS AND THE COMMUNITY

A further consequence of ERA is the increased right of choice and representation awarded to parents. Moreover, LEA financial cut-backs have resulted in parents becoming increasingly involved in fund-raising. This, coupled with the new market-orientated approach that encourages schools to seek support and sponsorships from local industry and commerce, has resulted in schools making greater efforts than before to foster links and form positive relations with its local community. In Smith's words, 'schools must be responsive to the community, not isolationist!' Even in western Canada – beyond the long shadow of ERA – Keerak notes the risks inherent in sponsorship whereby a school inadvertently becomes 'the advertising agency for any one business'. She describes how 70 per cent of the local taxpayers have no children in the school system. In order 'to ensure their ongoing support for funding public education or to enhance the possibility of their positive response at times when there is a call for public money for building expansions, it is crucial that they value the school'. McDonnell's perspective from his newly formed school is somewhat different: he makes the point that a primary school 'is a focal point for a community that may have little else in common . . . this is their new shared ground where, for a specific reason – the supported education of their children – they come day by day and begin to form new relationships'. The relationships between the school, its parents and the wider community are described by several contributors in terms of both giving and receiving. The support (both moral and material) of the community for the school is sought and, in a number of cases, the school premises are used by the community at evening or weekends. McDonnell is aware of the pastoral needs of some parents while he, Jones and Wilcock welcome parents as helpers in the school. Morton obtains parents' views on which areas need more attention and what more information on their child's education they want, while Smith involves parents in her paired-reading scheme.

In many ways, the changed relationship between schools and parents is one of the most positive developments in British education in recent years. The traditional mistrust that encouraged teachers to resist those parents who wished to spend time in their children's classes has largely given way to an intention in some, but by no means all, schools to get involved. On the other side of the coin, many parents are happy to respond to invitations to visit the school informally as well as for more formal occasions.

The parent–teacher relationship is a partnership. A survey of parental involvement carried out in the late 1980s by the National Foundation for Educational Research[2] illustrates how effective this partnership can be. This is not to say that all difficulties have been overcome: there can still be problems where a school has not established a clear policy for dealing with problems when they arise – when there is a clash of personality or when one party upsets the other, for example. But in general, where clearly thought-out policies have been formulated and agreed, the benefits to pupil learning are clear. Research has demonstrated this link and has shown (as in the famous Haringey study by Jack Tizard and colleagues)[3] that parental reading schemes can be more effective even than extra teaching.

CHALLENGE

All new heads face challenges and this group are no exception. But in addition to the (doubtless not uncommon) situation of long-serving staff fearing disruption of comfortable routines or of low staff morale following a period of uncertainty, a number of these primary headteachers had their early days in post dominated by the teachers' national industrial action of the mid-1980s. Furthermore, all but Keerak have been tested by the volume of paperwork and strictures subsequent upon the implementation of ERA. In the face of what many would see as a daunting, uphill task, they manifest a remarkable degree of optimism, enthusiasm and commitment. What emerges from these reflections on headship is the sustaining power of their feeling that, as head, they can achieve change: 'they can get things done'. The rewards they derive from working with young people – enabling them to experience, in McDonnell's words, 'effective and enjoyable learning' are clearly considerable.

That so many of these headteachers are positive is worthy of celebration. That so many of them gain satisfaction from – indeed, consider it a privilege to be involved in – supporting pupils' learning, is reassuring. Whether, in the interval between their completion of their chapters and the publication of this book their positive attitudes have been sustained can only be the subject of speculation. Readers, however, will need to relate what they have read here to the views of other headteachers with whom they are in contact.

What research into primary schools has shown is that the influence of the school on the development and academic progress of pupils can be strong. It appears this influence can even outweigh that of home background when *progress over time* rather than attainment at one point in time is concerned. This places a supreme importance on the role of the school and, therefore, on the role of the headteacher – the conductor of the orchestra – the one who leads, co-ordinates and liaises with all the players in order to achieve the best possible progress for the pupils. We end this chapter and this collection with a tribute to these and all the other headteachers of primary schools who are conducting similar orchestras and, therefore, working on behalf of the nation's most precious asset: its future generations.

NOTES

1. H.M. Senior Inspector of Schools (1991) *Standards in Education 1989–90*, HMI/ DES, London.
2. Jowett, S. and Baginsky, M. with MacDonald MacNeil, M. (1991) *Building Bridges: Parental Involvement in Schools*, NFER, Windsor.
3. Tizard, J., Schofield, W. and Hewison, J. (1982) Collaboration between teachers and parents in assisting children's reading, *British Journal of Educational Psychology*, Vol. 52, Part 1, pp. 1–15.

Index